Foundations of Modern History

Foundations of Modern History*
already published

*A. Goodwin, Emeritus Professor of Modern History, University of Manchester.
General Editor of this series until his retirement from the position in 1975.

The Emergence of the British Two-Party System 1760–1832

Frank O'Gorman
Senior Lecturer in History, University of Manchester

Edward Arnold

©Frank O'Gorman 1982

First published 1982 by
Edward Arnold (Publishers) Ltd
41 Bedford Square, London WC1B 3DQ

British Library Cataloguing in Publication Data

O'Gorman, Frank
   The emergence of the British two-party system
   1760-1832.—(Foundations of modern history)
   1. Political parties—Great Britain—History
   I. Title   II. Series
   324.241'02   JN1118

   ISBN 0-7131-6293-7

Text set in 10/11pt Baskerville Compugraphic by Colset Private Limited, Singapore
Printed and bound in Great Britain by Richard Clay (The Chaucer Press) Ltd,
Bungay, Suffolk

Contents

To Adam

Preface

In preparing this short book for publication I have become conscious of the debt which I owe to many historians who have reflected upon the problems dealt with in these pages. In a volume of this nature, however, detailed scholarly confrontations might be deemed redundant. I wish to express my gratitude to the unnamed scholars, therefore, who in the last two decades have begun to make sense of one of the most awkward and most neglected periods in modern British history. In the end, however, I encountered certain areas and topics which had not been thoroughly illuminated by modern research and I was driven back upon my own resources.

I am indebted to Mr E.A. Smith of the School of History in the University of Reading who was kind enough to read the book in typescript and to make many pertinent suggestions. For what follows, however, the author is entirely responsible.

Frank O'Gorman
University of Manchester
November 1981

Introduction

The predominance of two parties in politics has been a consistent feature of British life since the early nineteenth century. The subsequent achievements of Great Britain, the establishment of a liberal–democratic state, the preservation of political stability and the enlargement of civil and religious liberties, have owed much to the party-political framework within which they have emerged. Strangely, the development of this 'two-party system' has received little attention and the combination of circumstances which facilitated its emergence remains obscure. The purpose of this book is to describe and to illuminate this process, to provide a coherent interpretation of the emergence of the two-party system, to inform the general reader and to provoke the student to further enquiry. It does not pretend to provide a 'definitive' account of this, of all topics, in modern British history.

The essence of the British two-party system has been the competition for popular approval and the conflict for power at local as well as national level.[1] A third or even a fourth party may appear for a time upon the political stage but such parties usually lack the staying power, as well as the wide popular support, of the great parties. The idea of a 'two-party system' may even tolerate lengthy periods of one-party rule in which the oppositon party is unable to mount a successful challenge. Similarly, the two-party system has not been a fixed and static structure. Political catastrophes have forced realignments of parties from time to time while the rise of new social groups and the development of new social forces have summoned new parties into existence

---

[1] Definitional problems relating to party are particularly treacherous. Because it may be misleading to treat politics in terms of a party system I should explain my own understanding of what constitutes a party. In British history a party is an organized group which pursues political power and thus political office. It endeavours to cultivate popular support for its beliefs and focuses its activities upon Parliament. Such a definition satisfactorily distinguishes a party from a pressure group (such as the Anti-Corn Law League) and from a sectional group (such as the Irish Nationalists). Furthermore, such a definition is sufficiently flexible to allow parties to be treated (at the same or different times) as vehicles of ideology, agencies for securing popular support, dispensers of patronage or instruments of government. Parties are to be distinguished from factions (a) in the scope of their legislative and executive ambitions, (b) in the size of their parliamentary membership and the range of their popular support, (c) in their possession of an ideology of wide-ranging application.

from among the ashes of the old. Such realignments of party have usually operated, however, within a two-party framework. After each period of change and uncertainty politics resumes its normal two-party duality.

The theme of this book is that this characteristic duality makes its appearance in the 50 years before the Reform Act of 1832. By the 1830s the Whig and Tory parties had come to dominate Parliament, they had developed distinctive ideologies and programmes and they had begun to compete with each other in seeking popular approval for their proposals both at and between elections[2] thus they had come to dominate politics. Some elements of this general development had been anticipated in the 'Rage of Party' which historians attribute to the reigns of William III and of Anne but in the middle decades of the eighteenth century the impetus had been lost and some critical threads of continuity broken.

Once the central issues of Anne's reign, the succession, the established religion of the state and the security of the country, had been settled there was little to be Whig and Tory about. Party was identified with the instability and political ferment of the time and was consequently discredited. In the middle of the eighteenth century party labels were confined to the constituencies, where they lingered to give a cloak of respectability to traditional family conflicts and to provide an appeal to the electorate. At the national level, the prevailing political structure left no room for party. In mid century, the crucial political distinctions were those between supporters of government and of opposition, neither group professing a party ideology. Indeed, they were separated as much by their contrasting attitudes to power as by any party ideologies which they may have professed. Thus, opponents of the court customarily adopted the old 'country' sentiments which condemned the crude engrossment of office and sinecures, repudiated the political values which condoned corruption and nepotism in government and advocated a closer identification of government with opinion out of doors. In between the opposing forces of the supporters of government and opposition, however, stood a large number of independent men who were anxious to keep their distance of both. In fact, there were no national party organizations either inside Parliament or out in the country at general elections.[3] The tranquility

[2] Elections were held in 1802, 1806, 1807, 1812, 1818, 1820, 1826, 1830, 1831, 1832, 1835, 1837, 1841. In 39 years, therefore, there were no fewer than 13 elections. In the previous 39 there had been only six.

[3] In the last few years, historians have begun to qualify this kind of assertion. The Tories, proscribed from office by Walpole and George I and George II, nevertheless kept themselves together with some semblances of formal organization at Westminster and some very faint echoes of electoral organization. Although the Tories were almost always to be found in opposition, we should not imagine that a Government (Whig) *v.* Opposition (Tory) dichotomy existed. The effective leaders of oppositions were usually Whigs and, indeed, the Tories accepted most aspects of the Hanoverian establishment.

of politics in the mid eighteenth century was evidence of the death of
the old, religiously based politics of the earlier period. Such a period of
consensus, however, *made possible* the gradual, albeit intermittent,
emergence of a new and more stable form of party politics which was to
rest upon a general acceptance of the eighteenth-century Whig virtues
of parliamentary government. Then in the 50 years before the Reform
Act the trend towards two-party politics revived and became
irreversible.

Why did this happen? The answer to such a question must inevitably
extend far beyond the traditional boundaries of 'political' history and
into the dramatic social and economic changes of the period. More
specifically, attention should focus upon the interplay of a deepening
political consciousness with a long-standing tradition of political
assertiveness. The rise of new and the revival of old constitutional
concerns – especially those touching upon the religious organization
of the state – could hardly be ignored. The rising tide of political
debate and concern flooded into the existing political channels – of
elections, of parties, of opposition, of protest, petition and propaganda
– bringing an upsurge of vigour and new initiatives. The pressures for
political change may have been new but the mechanisms and techniques were largely traditional, the product of an earlier age of party
warfare and political and parliamentary conflict.

The evolution of parties and party systems, however, is never a
steady and gradual development. Certain periods of profound political
instability – the early 1760s, 1779–84, 1792–4, 1806–12, 1827–32
– provoked dramatic innovation, party realignment and political ferment. The intervening periods witness, at best, modest consolidation,
at worst, occasional retrogression. Why the phenomenon of political
instability should promote party development is in part explained by
the nature of instability itself. During a period of instability a society
throws into question one or more of its most basic beliefs or assumptions. It is around exactly such issues that parties form and prosper,
divide and realign. Thus, in the 1760s the role of the monarchy in
politics became a serious, central political issue for the first time in half
a century. In the late 1770s the issue of parliamentary sovereignty over
the American colonies and in the early 1780s the question of parliamentary reform provided rallying points for politicians. In the early
1790s the question of reform in general underwent a startling revival
through the impact of the French Revolution on British society and
created serious fissures in the Whig party. In the early years of the new
century, once again, the question of royal power and now, ominously,
the question of religious toleration, aggravated political alignments.
Finally, on the eve of the Reform Act of 1832, the twin issues of the
religious constitution of the state and the question of parliamentary
reform agitated politics and divided both parties.

In the course of this book we shall frequently investigate this relationship between political instability and party development. What we might notice here is that because they are a response to problems of instability, parties and party systems go far towards composing and thus confining such threats to the political establishment of the state. Indeed, since party politics constitute a general and sustained attempt to acquire not merely political but also judicial, military and economic power in the state, then party tends, on the whole, to conserve and perpetuate existing institutions. The emergence of a party system, therefore, constitutes a sophisticated agency of continuity and conservation of British institutions, practices and, not least, attitudes.

In the British case, the thrust of party government was in the direction of *parliamentary* government. By the early nineteenth century, Parliament was no longer simply a sovereign court of appeal nor essentially a legislative barrier to the pretensions of the executive but a legitimate instrument of executive power. In this sense a government with the support of a majority in both houses could proceed to translate its political intentions into practice. The idea of government *through* Parliament replaced that of government *limited* by Parliament. Consequently, British parties have for the most been parliamentary in character. It is moreover, I think, indisputable that because Parliament has been the unrivalled national political arena, the powerful local, centrifugal tendencies in British political life have been contained and curtailed. Party politics has consequently gone far towards harmonizing and unifying the varied elements, national, religious, regional, local, in the British political scene. By the 1830s it had become evident that the British state was to be founded upon a two-party system of politics. The ideologies, the traditions, the mentalities, the techniques and, to some extent, the organization of a two-party system had been fashioned. In spite of some retardations, the argument for a party political system of limited democracy had been won. Much that has been of significance in the history of Britain in the last century and a half has flowed from that reality, especially the fundamental stability and continuity of the country and its institutions.

1 The Revival of a Whig Party: 1760-1812

The Crucible of Party: 1760-82

The development of a party system in the later Hanoverian period was closely associated with the decline of political stability, an intermittent though generally accelerating feature of the times. The stability of the age of Walpole and the Pelhams had been no accident. It had rested upon three foundations. First, it had rested upon the monarch's acquiescence in the one-party rule of the Whigs and the corresponding proscription of the Tories from office. Second, it had depended upon the external security of the United Kingdom and the integrity of the British Empire, especially from the threat of the Bourbon powers. Third, it had proceeded from the internal ascendancy of the Protestant religion over the Dissenters and the Catholics, especially the Irish Catholics. By 1782 all three of these bulwarks of stability had been weakened in varying degrees. Public agitation of these fundamentals gave rise to furious controversy and thus to a revival and intensification of party conflict. In the 1760s the first of these fundamental preconditions for stability, the relationship between the King, the Whigs and the Tories, could no longer be taken for granted. It is in this that the revival of party has its origin.

On his accession to the throne in 1760, George III was already determined to free the monarchy from what he took to be its servitude to the Whigs, especially the old corps Whigs, and to form his administrations from the best men of all parties. The bogey of Jacobitism, with which Walpole and the Pelhams had terrified the first two Hanoverian monarchs into employing old corps Whigs and proscribing the crypto-Jacobite Tories, meant nothing to him. By 1760, moreover, the Whigs were no longer motivated by any particular conception of party. The death of Henry Pelham in 1754 had already left them vulnerable to their own family and factional divisions (which the Seven Years War, 1756-63, had restrained), and to William Pitt the Elder's political arts and ambitions (which the Seven Years War had enhanced). During the war, however, Pitt began what George III was to conclude, the ending of the proscription of the Tories. Pitt gave them commissions in the new county militia. George III ended their symbolic banishment from the court and brought them, as individuals, back within the political pale. In the early years of the new reign, the old Tory party, long since consigned to the parliamentary back benches, finally expired. What was left of its membership fragmented, some attaching themselves to the court, others to the Elder Pitt, still others to alternative political leaders while yet others preferred to maintain a lofty yet lonely position of honourable independence. The long agonies of the old Tory party were at last brought to an end.

But the crisis of the old corps Whigs was only beginning. George III hated them and their political arts and he was determined to play the political game according to rules which his two predecessors would never have recognized. With his tutor and mentor, the Earl of Bute, at his side, neither Pitt, the Secretary of State, nor Newcastle, the First Lord of the Treasury, could enjoy a frank and confidential relationship with the monarch. The King and Bute proceeded to welcome, although they did not instigate, the resignations of Pitt (October 1761) and Newcastle (May 1762). The resignations, in fact, had their origin in internal cabinet divisions on the management of the war but they unquestionably enhanced the power and influence of the favourite. Bute became First Lord of the Treasury after the fall of Newcastle. By now the stakes were high. The King and Bute would brook no opposition in their endeavours to negotiate peace, in late 1762 the touchstone of political allegiance. The refusal of Newcastle and the old Whigs to support the Peace Preliminaries in Parliament in December 1762 led to savage reprisals. In the 'Massacre of the Pelhamite Innocents' in the winter of 1762–3 the friends of Newcastle were systematically removed from their offices in local and county government. The victory of George III and the humiliation of the old Whigs seemed complete.

It was, perhaps, natural for their resentment against Bute to swell into a thoroughgoing condemnation of the politics of 'secret influence'. When Bute resigned the Treasury in April 1763, for example, his political influence did not thereby terminate. He remained on good terms with the King and helped with the establishment of the Grenville ministry. Although without office, and thus without formal responsibility, he retained the King's confidence. The Newcastle Whigs vied with each other in their vigorous denunciations of his 'unconstitutional' situation as 'Minister behind the Curtain'. The fact that Bute was a Scot and a Stuart, as well as the reported lover of the Princess Dowager, made him an ideal scapegoat. The myth of Lord Bute's 'secret influence' became a satisfying and compelling, albeit retrospective, explanation of the politics of the new reign. By late 1763, the Newcastle Whigs were claiming that Bute had seduced the King into conspiring in a plot to undermine the aristocracy and to destroy the old corps Whigs. Bute and certain sinister creatures around him, so the argument ran, wished to elevate the banner of prerogative in the guise of 'secret influence'. Government by favourite would effectively leave no check and no curb upon those who manipulated royal power because the traditional check exercised by Parliament would be set at nought.

Was the 'Bute Myth' nothing more than an exaggerated justification by which disappointed politicians, accustomed to office, vindicated their attempts to clamber back into power? It is certainly the case that the conversion of the Newcastle Whigs from the traditional Pelhamite nostrums of service to the court, which they were still uttering in the spring of 1762, to the full-blown fantasy of the 'Bute Myth', was a rapid development but they seem sincerely to have been frightened of Bute. Furthermore, the old corps had never been passive instruments of monarchy. In office, they had preached the doctrine of government by connection and assigned to themselves the roles of custodians of the Whig tradition of limited monarchy. They unquestionably believed that they should serve the monarchy but neither unreservedly nor indiscriminately. In some senses, then, the anti-court rhetoric in which the Newcastle Whigs began to indulge in the summer of 1763 was less inconsistent with their earlier traditions of service to the court than might at first appear.

Whatever its status, the 'Bute Myth' occupies a critically important place in Whig history. It facilitated the agonizing transformation of habits which the Newcastle Whigs were to effect, from those of office to those of opposition. It was the 'Bute Myth' which established that central preoccupation in the minds of those opposed to George III, 'secret influence'. What is so interesting about the 'Bute Myth' is its elasticity. It could be called upon to explain any reverse, any failure, any humiliation. But, more than that, it could explain any abuse of government, any accident of power. It was the key to understanding the politics of the reign and one which both eased and legitimized Whig opposition to the monarchy and the ministers of George III.

Indeed, it was to be within this framework of perceptions that the Newcastle Whigs waged their somewhat tentative war against the court during the next few years. At once, a new authoritarian tone appeared in the savagery of the Grenville ministry's attack upon John Wilkes.[1] Newcastle sought the co-operation of Pitt in resisting the new

[1] John Wilkes had been MP for Aylesbury since 1757. In his weekly paper, *The North Briton*, Wilkes had consistently attacked the Bute Ministry. His celebrated and scandalous writings represent the most extravagant version of the 'Bute Myth'. In the famous 45th issue published on 19 April 1763 Wilkes outdid himself, dismissing the Peace of Paris as a humiliating surrender, denouncing the cabinet as servile tools of the favourite and strongly hinting that the King was a helpless prisoner. Wilkes was thrown into prison and his belongings seized, following the issue of a General Warrant. Forty-nine other persons were seized with Wilkes. Later in the year, Parliament voted its approval

high-handedness of the court. His failure forced his friends to organize themselves into a more effective parliamentary opposition. The organization of Wildman's Club in the winter of 1763–4 acted as the catalyst for a direct challenge to the administration. In spite of the hesitations of Newcastle and the old guard, Wildman's and the younger men who were the force behind it whipped in Opposition and Independent members for a full-scale assault on the ministry on the issue of General Warrants. Although Grenville survived the attack in February 1764, the Newcastle Whigs had advanced one stage further in their opposition to the court. Suspicions of the favourite had now been translated into a parliamentary challenge to the ministry of the King's choice. It is not without a certain ironical justice, therefore, that exactly at this time the extravagant fantasies about Bute's influence had their greatest justification. During the early months of the Grenville ministry Bute's influence behind the curtain was at its height. He was, for example, closely involved in detailed discussions for a change of ministry in the summer and autumn of 1763, leading none other than Grenville to demand that his interference should cease. No doubt the opposition exaggerated Bute's influence but there can be no doubt that they had put their finger upon a real rather than a fictitious issue in touching upon the principle of government by favourite.

The collapse of Grenville's ministry in 1765 and the refusal of Pitt to succeed him left the way clear for the Newcastle Whigs to return to office. During these critical, formative years of the Whig party few experiences affected them more deeply than their return to office.

For one thing, it marks the transfer of both formal and effective leadership to the Marquis of Rockingham. Rockingham was a rich Yorkshire aristocrat, much cultivated by Newcastle and the other Whig grandees, yet acceptable to all sections of the party, including the younger men within it. In some ways, Rockingham's provincial background was to be his most significant contribution to the Newcastle connection. It injected an element of country opinion into the Pelhamite traditions of aristocratic Whiggism and service to the court. Rockingham's monopoly of power in his Yorkshire kingdom enabled him to enjoy the support of Whigs of all descriptions, of Tories and of Independents. Here was a man in many respects very different from the Duke of Newcastle.

At the same time, the return to office of the Newcastle-Rockingham Whigs in 1765–6 confirmed the mutual suspicion that existed between themselves and the court, and deepened their antipathies towards

of these actions and, in addition, voted no. 45 a seditious libel, not covered by parliamentary privilege. On 19 January 1764 John Wilkes was expelled from the House of Commons.

Bute. George III was contemptuous of Rockingham's abilities and suspicious of his motives. His suspicions were thoroughly confirmed when Rockingham made him agree that Bute should have no influence during the ministry and persuaded him vaguely to promise to discipline office holders who might refuse to support the ministry. Ministers further offended the King by omitting to consult him over the great legislative enactment of the ministry, the Repeal of the Stamp Act, a dramatic confession of the failure of the mother country to raise taxes in America. (The King was in favour of some modification of the Act.) The passage of the American legislation inevitably caused the ministers some anxious moments. For these, they blamed the King, complaining of his lukewarm support and his reluctance to force recalcitrant office-holders to support the ministry. Constantly complaining of the weakness of the ministry and several times advising the monarch to send for Pitt, the Rockinghams could not consistently complain when, in the end, George did just that, replacing them with Pitt in July 1766.

They could, however, nurture their rapidly emerging hatred of 'the Great Commoner'. Pitt had done nothing to assist or sustain the ministry. Indeed, he had snatched the glory of declaring General Warrants illegal from their lips by extending the illegality from libels to all cases. Furthermore, in the last few months of its life Pitt had begun to attack the ministry, clearly wishing to profit from its weaknesses. When he began in Parliament to voice his admiration for Lord Bute Rockingham began to suspect a plot to install Pitt as an agent of the favourite.

It is to the modern mind perplexing that when Rockingham and a few leaders of the party resigned in July 1766 they did not sound the clarion call of opposition to their followers, who were thus permitted to remain in their places. In reality, it may not have been easy to persuade them to stand down, especially when the charismatic Pitt, their one-time colleague in office, had not enunciated any policy to which they might have taken exception. To keep his men in, moreover, might have given Rockingham some influence within a ministry which was dangerously talking the language of extirpating party. To have brought out his men might even have facilitated the designs of the court because hungry Buteites would no doubt have filled the vacant places. Even if Rockingham had declared open war on the court by calling his men out, he would only have succeeded in driving Bute and the King into the arms of Chatham (as Pitt now became). By November 1766, however, this uneasy compromise had collapsed. Chatham detested the presence of Rockinghamites within his ministry and could barely be civil to them. A stream of calculated insults culminated in the humiliating dismissal of a senior Rockinghamite, Lord Edgecumbe.

This was too much for Rockingham, who called upon his men to resign.

This final breach with Chatham was a disaster for the Rockinghams. At least 40 of them refused to sacrifice their political careers, thus throwing in their lot with Chatham and with the King. The Edgecumbe affair changed the nature of the Rockingham party. In losing their Chathamite and court wings they deprived themselves of half their number. After 1766 the Rockinghams were no longer a sprawling collection of old Pelhamites, Chathamites, ministerialists, Tories and Independents. The party was now more united in its fundamentals, central among which were resistance to the secret influence of Lord Bute and hostility to the anti-party ministry of Lord Chatham. If their political isolation left the régime of 'secret influence' undisturbed, Rockinghamites could congratulate themselves that they had safeguarded their political virtue and resisted the blandishments of the court. The wilderness of opposition seemed a demonstration as well as a corroboration of their political virtue.

It followed, however, that any effective crusade against the court required the Rockinghams to unite with other groups. This they attempted to do during 1767. The negotiations of that year for a reconstruction of Chatham's faltering ministry brought the Rockinghams to clarify their conditions for co-operation and thus to define the limits of their party thinking. What Rockingham had in mind was a coalition in which his own party would dominate, leading to a ministry in which the Treasury would be his and the major cabinet posts at the disposal of his party, indeed, filled by his appointees. Rockingham had learned the lesson of his first ministry. His party would by itself be too weak to stand, but *assisted* by other groups, *led* by his own, a broad-based ministry would be too strong to be resisted, even by Lord Bute. The purpose of a future party administration would be avowedly to destroy the system of 'secret influence'. Given these conditions, the failure of the negotiations was only to be expected.

By 1768 the essential features of the Rockingham Whig party had clearly emerged. But what relationship did this party bear to that of the Duke of Newcastle and, indeed, to the old corps of the reign of George II? Alternatively, to what extent were the Rockingham Whigs a new party?

So far as individuals are concerned, it is possible to demonstrate a considerable measure of continuity between the Newcastle and Rockingham Whigs. Two-thirds of the Rockingham Whigs who fought the General Election of 1768 had supported the Duke of Newcastle in his opposition to George Grenville's administration in 1764. Of the Newcastle Whigs who can be identified in 1764, when the size of his group had emerged with some consistency at something over 100, slightly less than half of those remaining in politics in 1768 supported Rockingham. That so many old Pelhamites should have sought refuge at court, especially during the Chatham administration, should occasion little surprise. The old corps had been characterized by strong traditions of service to the monarchy and the Rockingham Whigs were treading contentious ground in condemning Chatham, Bute, and, indeed, the general system of politics practised by the court in the new reign.

It is possible, similarly, to identify ideological connections between the old corps, the Newcastle Whigs and the party of the Marquis of Rockingham. The old corps had assumed, rightly or wrongly, that they were the custodians of Whiggism and the heirs of the Revolution families. They had insisted that a 'Tory' threat to the constitution existed which it was for 'the Whigs' to resist. They had, moreover, demonstrated that while the King should be respected, and his prerogatives preserved intact, in practice, ministers should govern. These traditions the Rockinghams inherited but grafted them onto certain key attitudes derived from country party hostility to courts and courtiers. Such ancient political chords had been struck against ministers and monarchs since the early seventeenth century. The notes were the same: disapproval of corruption, opposition to wasteful expenditure and a firm tendency, manifest in the First Rockingham ministry's exertions to carry the mercantile interest with it over its American policy, to consult public opinion. A fresh synthesis of Whig principles was in the process of emerging.

It was these ideas that Edmund Burke was to fashion into a new version of Whiggism and into a theory of party at the end of the decade. His influence within the Rockingham party has traditionally been exaggerated. He was very much the servant of the Marquis of Rockingham and very far from being his master. He did not come into the Rockingham party in 1766 to endow it with a ready-made theory of party. He derived his ideas from their experiences, to some extent from their grudges. Thus in 1769 he published a severely anti-Grenvillite work, *Observations on a Late Publication intituled The Present State of the Nation*. In April 1770 he issued his most famous work on party, *Thoughts on the Cause of the Present Discontents*, patently an anti-Chathamite polemic. He proclaimed in *Thoughts* the superior value of acting collectively in party to the dependence of individuals upon the transient abilities of one man. The Chatham administration, always an unreal and impractical anti-party crusade, had collapsed in 1768 and, a year later, Chatham was drifting into a systematic opposition to the new ministry, led by the Duke of Grafton. In the ensuing power struggle between Rockingham and Chatham for leadership of the opposition, the Rockinghams were anxious to vindicate both their past and present conduct.

Burke's idea of party was thus an attack upon Chatham's repudiation of party, an affirmation of the politics of the landed Whig aristocracy against the 'Patriotic' values of the 'Great Commoner'. Burke may have entered the political scene just too late to catch the full force of Newcastle's fear of Bute but he was just in time to share Rockingham's bitter resentment at Pitt's refusal to help them during the ministry of 1765–6 and his own party's shock over the Edgecumbe affair. Now, in the very different political world of 1769–70 Chatham must once again be kept at bay. While Burke was writing the *Thoughts* the Petitioning Movement of 1769 was proceeding apace, to culminate, the Rockinghams hoped, in the fall of the Grafton ministry, and its replacement by a grand coalition ministry. But who was to lead it and what should be its personnel as well as its purposes? To the debate provoked by questions such as these, Burke directed his party writings.

More important, however, Burke's party theory was a repudiation of the politics of the court. This was far more than personal mistrust of Bute. The Rockinghams were opposing the court not because of *Bute's* influence but because of the *system* of government which Bute had allegedly established. In 1767, for example, the Rockinghams had resisted the East India policy of the Chatham administration because 'secret influence' threatened to expand the province of government and subvert the rights of property. Consequently, the party had leapt to the defence of the chartered rights of the Company. By 1770 government by party was the Rockinghams' alternative to government by 'secret influence'. Bute may no longer have been the personal threat that he had been but 'His System is got into firmer and abler hands.'[2]

Burke wished to revert to what he imagined had been the political practices of the reigns of George I and II when a powerful Whig aristocracy had governed the country, acting as the custodian of its liberties, enjoying the exercise of royal powers and the implementation of royal prerogatives in suppressing the twin and related threats of Toryism and Jacobitism. In elaborating his theory of party, therefore, Burke

---

[2] Burke to Rockingham, 29 December 1770, *Burke Correspondence*, ed. Lucy M. Sutherland (1960) II, pp. 174–6. The work was also intended to unite and strengthen the Rockingham Whigs by publicizing their justification of themselves and thus stating their principles. 'I think it would take universally, and tend to form and to unite a party upon real and well founded principles', wrote Rockingham to Burke, 15 October 1769, *Correspondence*, p. 92. The Rockinghams have been ridiculed for their alarmism where Bute was concerned but there is more to be said on their behalf than is frequently allowed. After all, Bute's position during the Grenville ministry *had* been exceptional. There is evidence, moreover, that the relationship between the King and the favourite persisted not only during the Rockingham ministry of 1765–6 but even as late as 1767, when the King was receiving Bute's advice about the ministerial negotiations of that year.

was claiming traditional Whig principles for the Rockinghams. As he wrote in 1791, 'When he entered into the Whig party, he did not conceive that they pretended to any discoveries.' For Burke it was the duty of good Whigs to preserve the constitution, protect the Hanoverian succession, and, in their natural function as leaders of society, govern the country by counselling the King.

It followed that the Rockingham party ought to seek power through constitutional means. It should not seek to engross power and offices in a mean and exclusive spirit but should admit 'healing coalitions' so long as they did not contradict fundamental party principles. Party men must fill the great offices of state, moreover, and rest their measures upon parliamentary approval and public consent. Until they were able to form a government, party men should act together in opposing unconstitutional measures and in resisting systems of government which threatened the spirit of the constitution.

Edmund Burke wished party to be the vehicle of political regeneration. He wished to restore an old polity and reinstate traditional values. He did not wish to invent new ones. He wished to compose differences in the state not to elaborate a party manifesto. Consequently, Burke has nothing to say about the organization of party nor the institutionalization of its activities. He was scarcely interested in strengthening the party out of doors through improved electoral and organizational techniques. Similarly, he never seems to have considered the possibility of improving the numerical strength of the Rockingham party within Parliament. Indeed, when such developments occurred in the 1780s Burke had nothing to do with them. Burke did not conceive of party within a developing constitutional framework. The idea that the British political system might move towards a two-party system of government was entirely absent from his thinking. The restoration of the constitution which Burke envisaged was to be achieved not through the institutionalization of political conflict but through the virtuous exertions of party men in eliminating the system of secret influence.

The formulation of Edmund Burke's party theories was an important step in enhancing the legitimacy of party activity *in opposition*. More particularly, it sharply defined the political values of the Rockingham Whigs and served to distinguish them from other political groups. In particular, it went far towards weakening their relationship with Chatham. Their co-operation in 1769 in defence of John Wilkes and the rights of electors[3] had never been more than lukewarm. Chatham took a more libertarian view of events than the

[3] Wilkes's election to Parliament as MP for Middlesex had been set aside by the Commons, which voted to deprive him of his seat in February 1769. They proceeded to permit the election of his beaten opponent, Luttrell, even though Wilkes thrice defeated him in successive elections.

Rockinghams who, characteristically, leapt to the conclusion that the court system was now threatening hitherto sacrosanct rights. Nevertheless, Chatham retained enormous public respect which the Rockinghams could not afford to despise. Yet, as we have seen, Rockingham's objective was to shake the Grafton ministry and to succeed it with a united administration led by himself. How his attitude towards Chatham had changed since the humiliating endeavours to obtain his support in 1765–6. Chatham further affronted Rockingham by making a dramatic bid for popular and radical support in the metropolis by committing himself to Parliamentary Reform in January 1770. In short, the publication of the *Thoughts* simply underlined the difficulties in the way of co-operation. It did not cause them. Although talk of a 'union of the opposition' continued for a while, it was all but dead by 1772. At bottom, they appreciated different political values: Chatham those of the individual in politics, the Rockinghams those of mutual co-operation in party. As Rockingham's suspicion of 'secret influence' became ever stronger[4] Chatham's irritation with the hesitant gang of cliquish aristocrats was difficult to restrain.

We noted at the outset that the stability of the mid eighteenth century had been founded upon monarchical acquiescence in Whig rule. By the early 1770s, George III's desire to play a more active political role had disturbed that stability and, indirectly, contributed to the emergence of a Rockingham Whig party. Its life in the next 10 years was to be dominated by the erosion of the second great foundation of stability, the integrity of the British Empire and the security of the country. As early as the Rockingham Ministry of 1765–6, the Rockinghams had been prepared to defy the King and to repeal the Stamp Act, passed by George Grenville just a year earlier, and designed to elicit a revenue from the American colonists. Nevertheless, the American policy of this ministry was not informed by any unique, liberal approach to imperial government. To repeal the Stamp Act was simply common sense, although it might make for embarrassments at home. In any case, the repeal was accompanied by a Declaratory Act which clearly affirmed the right of the British Parliament to tax the colonies. Thereafter, the American policy of the Rockingham party in opposition was an amalgamation of good intentions, indifference,

---

[4] It was not merely the drift of imperial policy which worried the Rockinghams in the 1770s. Attacks on the rights of juries and the independence of printers in the early years of the decade seemed to indicate an extension of 'secret influence'. Furthermore, the Royal Marriages Act of 1772, requiring the consent of the monarch to a marriage by a member of the royal family, was regarded by them as a dangerous constitutional innovation which gave statutory extension to the royal prerogative. On many of these issues Chatham adopted a very different approach and never accepted the Rockinghamites' fear of 'secret influence'.

political opportunism and, not least, a persisting inclination to restrain the court from corrupting the empire with its untrustworthy system of 'secret influence'.

Thus, as armed conflict between the mother country and the colonists approached in the 1770s, Rockinghamite attitudes remained frozen within a framework of imperial relationships dominated by the Declaratory Act and the fear of secret influence. This was why Rockinghamite attitudes had such a pacificist tendency. War was unthinkable because the increase of civil and military establishments would expand the dangerously increasing engines of 'secret influence'. Burke and his party were thus ready to go to almost any lengths to maintain even a fig-leaf of respectability for the Declaratory Act in their successive Conciliation speeches and proposals. This policy was at bottom contradictory for Conciliation could not succeed so long as the Declaratory Act was maintained. Even the Declaration of American Independence, however, failed to budge the Rockinghams. After war had commenced they continued, nobly but in vain, to preach the virtues of Conciliation. For political reasons they could not afford to attack the principle of a war which was being fought to protect the rights of Parliament over the colonies and it was not until the failure of British arms that the Rockinghams came to accept the inevitability of American Independence. To resist it indefinitely would not merely reinforce executive power; it would lead to national disaster, as the Bourbon powers joined in the war on the side of the Americans in 1778. Thus the Rockinghams in the end came to regard Washington's armies as allies in the fight against 'secret influence'.

Purely from the point of view of the evolution of the Rockingham party, moreover, the American issue led to the extension of the claims of party. Political and constitutional differences between the government of Lord North (1770–82) and the Rockinghams became so complete that by 1780 they were calling for his resignation, advocating American Independence and, most significantly, demanding a dominant place in the composition of the next government. This amounted, in practice, to a challenge to the royal prerogative of appointing ministers. At first, such a challenge seemed both imprudent and unpopular. By the time that the North ministry had finally discredited itself, however, with the colonies lost, half the powers of Europe at war with Britain, Ireland in turmoil and a rising spirit of radicalism threatening to disrupt domestic security, the Rockinghamites' platform seemed both statesmanlike and prophetic. The American War may have kept the Rockinghams out of office and consigned them to years of frustratingly impotent opposition, but in the end it rescued their reputations, vindicated their opposition and legitimated the role of party in the state.

In the longer term, the most influential of the divisive issues raised by the American War, and unquestionably that which was to have the greatest impact upon the party's long-term fortunes, was reform. The issue of parliamentary sovereignty, the principle of 'No Taxation without Representation', the military disasters and the administrative incompetence revealed by the war conspired to raise the issues of parliamentary and Economical (or administrative) reform, while encouraging the conditions for the spread of radical ideas. In the winter of 1779–80 an ominous Petitioning Movement, organized by county committees, appeared, led by Christopher Wyvill, a Yorkshire clergyman. The Movement expressed the anxieties and the aspirations of the county freeholders and urban middling orders during an unsuccessful war. They protested against high taxation, administrative incompetence, extravagance and negligence in government and, consequently, advocated Economical Reform i.e. legislation to limit the number of offices at the disposal of the Crown. Noting, however, the inability of Parliament to check the executive and its constant support for North's ministry, the Movement demanded triennial Parliaments and a reformed franchise.[5]

The Rockinghams could not ignore what Wyvill was preaching. They agreed with him on Economical Reform. Indeed, insofar as it reflected the instinctive 'country' attitudes of the independents and freeholders of the counties, the Petitioning Movement coincided with the country elements in Rockinghamite thinking. But they could not accept the need for parliamentary reform. It was not just that the Rockinghams wished to defend their boroughs and their landed political influence. They sincerely believed that the radical cures would make the patient worse and, in weakening *aristocratic* power, permit royal influence to rise unchecked. For the present, however, the Rockinghams had no alternative but to work with the Movement and, if possible, to prevent it from going to extremes. Thus the rising wave of radical agitation in the country in the spring and summer of 1780 reinforced the parliamentary campaigns of the Rockinghams as they endeavoured to carry Economical reform. Their failure to do so is not surprising in view of the enormous majorities which North's ministry still enjoyed. Indeed, it is much to their credit that they made North

[5] Already by 1770 Burke had been aware that the radicals associated with Wilkes had come to agree with the Rockinghamite diagnosis of 'secret influence' but he noted with alarm that they disagreed over the cure. Instead of party government, the radicals advocated far-reaching constitutional changes which, in Burke's view, would have disastrous consequences. This is why in the *Thoughts* Burke goes out of his way to reject radical proposals, e.g. more frequent elections would enable the court to practise its corruption more frequently and with more fatal effect. For Burke, the traditional institutions of the constitution did not need to change. The traditional practices of the constitution needed to be vindicated.

fight for his life and ultimately negotiate with them. Furthermore, the experience of 1780 encouraged some of the younger and more enthusiastic men in the party, especially the radical circle around Charles James Fox, to proclaim that the House of Commons ought to be more responsive to the popular will. Such divisions distressed Rockingham, widened the gulf between his party and the Chathamites, led since Chatham's death in 1778 by Lord Shelburne, and ended any prospect there might have been that his party would have enjoyed the unreserved support of the Petitioning counties and towns at the general election of 1780. Here may be discerned the seeds of later discord and division. At the same time, it is salutary to note how far the Rockingham party had come since the early 1760s and the days of the Duke of Newcastle.

These were not auspicious years for an opposition. The task of opposition in the eighteenth century, always daunting in view of the enormous psychological as well as practical difficulties under which it had to labour – of communication, of attendance, of morale, of preparation – was arguably more difficult during the years of the American War than at most other periods in the century. The cause of Parliament's war seemed noble and the nation rallied around the throne. The Rockingham were, at times, indolent and on some issues they were divided. But then so were all oppositions, as well as most governments, of the century. Nevertheless, the Rockinghams continued to exploit the traditional technical, procedural and organizational opportunities open to opposition parties. Their involvement in petitions has been touched open. In 1769 they helped to frighten a ministry out of existence; in 1780 they brought another to its knees and forced it to negotiate. Their exploitation of divisions was carefully selective. Only after 1774 did they divide annually upon the Address. Similarly, they awaited their opportunity before moving Addresses to the Crown, motions of No Confidence and resolutions for a Committee on the State of the Nation. Of course, such stratagems had little chance of success. (The Rockinghams, 50–60 in 1766 rising to 80–90 in 1782, were far too few in number to endanger a ministry.) They were undertaken to attack the ministry, to maintain morale and consistency and to appeal to the public. During the war, they constantly demanded Papers and Accounts. They broke new ground in 1780 when they contested (unsuccessfully) the Speakership. They were also more conscientious than earlier oppositions had been at proposing legislation of their own. Finally, their ability to whip-in their followers should not be underestimated. In the Parliament of 1774–80 they averaged an 80 per cent attendance for the 12 issues for which Division Lists survive, comparing favourably, for example, with the attendance of the Tories earlier in the century.

There can be little doubt, therefore, that unusual significance attaches to the Rockingham Whig party. Arguably, certain other political groups have some claim to be regarded as a party during this period on the grounds of ideological consistency and organizational cohesion. But unlike the Bedford Whigs and Grenville Whigs, however, the Rockinghams gloried in their party principles, stood for party government and advocated party politics. Other groups were little more than tactical units which created little or nothing that was to endure in the history of party. In any case, the Rockinghams alone among the groups who may be considered to be parties endured. The Grenville Whigs failed to survive the death of their leader in 1770 and joined North's ministry. The Bedfords had already made their peace with the court in 1767. The Rockinghams, on the other hand, survived the dark years of opposition, when the normal paths to ministerial office had been closed off and when nothing short of a convulsive crisis could have brought them to office.

This, then, was the Rockinghams' achievement. They tended the delicate growth of party to survival and to vindication in 1782 in spite of their anti-Chathamite and, to some extent, anti-monarchical associations. They succeeded in laying the foundations for a new tradition of party while relating their work and their involvements to the party traditions of the past. By 1782 party had already become a refuge to which the nation might turn at a time of crisis. Few could have imagined that what followed between 1782 and 1784 would have had such far-reaching consequences as to have inspired nothing less than a new era in the history of party.

Cohesion and Crisis: 1782–94

These years witness the Whig party's dramatic challenge to the monarchy of George III, its failure at the general election of 1784, its further evolution and development in opposition thereafter and, under the impact of the French Revolution, its ultimate redefinition. The coalition of half the Whig party with the ministry of the Younger Pitt in 1794 by no means deprives these years of consequence. They are full of ideological and organizational innovation whose example and impact were to reverberate into the nineteenth century.

These developments were inaugurated by the prolonged constitutional crisis of 1782–4. The failure of British armies to subdue the American colonists provoked a reaction of public and parliamentary opinion which swept North from office in March 1782. From then until April 1784 the basic theme of British political history was the problem of establishing a ministry which enjoyed the confidence both of the King and of Parliament. The King was unable to impose his will on the men of the Rockingham party just as they were unable to impose their will on him. From the ensuing confusion flowed two years of political upheaval and ministerial instability.

The immediate result of the fall of North was a ministry composed of Rockingham's men in uneasy alliance with Shelburne's group. The unhappy history of this divided administration turns upon the King's determined and consistent repudiation of the principles of party. Although he was prepared to bow to the inevitable reversal of policy on American independence and Economical Reform in March 1782, he refused to acknowledge that a political party could dictate his appointment of ministers. Consequently, he was careful to treat Shelburne as a co-equal leader of the Rockingham ministry. George III had been prepared to work with Chatham in 1766 and now he was content to work with Chatham's disciple. Shelburne's adherence to Chathamite principles, which included the repudiation of party and the appointment of men by merit rather than connection, coincided with his own rising ambitions.

The Rockingham Whigs were the first victims of Shelburne's ambitions. Whatever hopes and illusions Rockingham may have cherished in the dark years of opposition after 1766 he found that he was unable to govern independently of the King, or, indeed, of Shelburne. Shelburne 'could not bear the idea of a *round-robin administration*, where the whole cabinet must be consulted for the disposal of the most trifling employments'. Contrary to Rockingham, he believed that business must be submitted to the King by departmental ministers before it came to the cabinet. Inevitably, every issue and every appointment became a battle for power and a test of constitutional principle. The Rockinghamite crusade for party evaporated in the carefully cultivated anarchy which the obduracy of the King and the manoeuvres of Shelburne created. When Rockingham died on 1 July 1782 and the King replaced him with Shelburne the crusade appeared to be over.

Political desperation drove Charles James Fox, after Rockingham's death the effective leader of his party, to declare that the appointment of Shelburne was illegitimate and to demand that the cabinet rather than the King appoint Rockingham's successor. Although the monarch would, no doubt, have been wise to have consulted the cabinet, whose leader had died in office, there was nothing to compel him to follow their recommendation. In any case, had he done so in July 1782 the cabinet would almost certainly have recommended Shelburne! It was the near impossibility – within the prevailing constitutional conventions – of establishing party government that led to Fox's desperate throw. Shelburne saw what was at stake: 'whether the executive is to be taken out of the King's hands and lodged, as Mr Fox says, in the hands of a party, or, to speak more truly, in his own.' Had

Fox acquiesced, however, in Shelburne's appointment he would have been tacitly acknowledging the principles of the King and of Shelburne. The political crisis was bringing into the open issues which had for years remained hypothetical and forcing politicians on all sides both to defend their ideas and to justify actions into which they were driven by the pressure of events.

The old mistrust of Chatham now revived in the quite extraordinary hatred evinced by the Rockingham party, now under the leadership of the Duke of Portland, for Shelburne. In the circumstances it seemed natural for Portland's men to negotiate a coalition with the followers of North as a means of bringing down the Shelburne ministry, which they did in the spring of 1783. The 'Fox–North coalition' was ridiculed by contemporaries and has since been criticized by historians, but it is difficult to see what alternative there was to it. Shelburne himself vetoed a coalition with North and a Shelburne–Fox coalition was quite unthinkable. If there were to be a stable ministry then a coalition of some sort was essential. There had never been any personal animosity between North and the Rockingham Whigs. They had never regarded him as they had once regarded Bute and Chatham – and now Shelburne – as a king's man, who would frustrate and who might even destroy their party. After all, the war in America had been fought to safeguard the rights of Parliament not those of the King. The old issues which had separated them from North had passed or were passing. Consequently there seemed to them nothing reprehensible or inconsistent about the Coalition. Indeed, the major stipulation of the agreement was that in a future Coalition ministry 'government by departments' as envisaged by Shelburne and George III would not be tolerated. The King, therefore, was forced by the parliamentary strength of the Coalition to give way to Fox and Portland. The Coalition came to power in the spring of 1783 as Portland forced on George III the most humiliating ministerial settlement ever accepted by a Hanoverian monarch. He conceded not merely Portland's cabinet list but *carte blanche* for the cabinet to appoint to junior positions.

The King was merely biding his time. The latent conflict in the eighteenth-century constitution between the powers of the monarch and those of a ministry which enjoyed the confidence of Parliament was now brutally apparent. To resolve that conflict required such an unusual exercise of royal power as even George III had never previously attempted. In December 1783 at George III's instigation the House of Lords voted down the ministry's India Bill. The status of his action and his subsequent refusal to bow to the wishes of a Commons majority and reinstate the Coalition became the touchstone of political allegiance for two decades and more.

In such a struggle, the leaders of both sides were careful to marshall their arguments in their endeavours to influence opinion both inside and outside Parliament. The Portland Whigs were particularly anxious lest they be outmanoeuvred once more by George III and rested their case on a Whiggish defence of the rights of Parliament. In the first place, Fox repudiated the legality of the means by which the King had overthrown the Coalition ministry. That ministry, enjoying the support of huge majorities in the Commons, had been brought down by means of sinister manoeuvres in the House of Lords. The ministry of Pitt stood, therefore, upon an illegitimate foundation. There could be no compromise with Pitt – or with the King – until that unconstitutionality had been conceded. Secondly, the Coalition rested their case squarely upon the rights of the Commons to advise the King on the exercise of the prerogative of appointing ministers and, in the last analysis, to refuse to support a minister of the King's choice. The string of defeats suffered by Pitt in the Commons during the winter of 1783–4 amounted, in the view of Portland, Fox, North and their supporters, to a repudiation of the rights of the Commons. 'What sort of government could take place on a principle which did not imply the confidence of the House?' demanded Fox. Finally, the Coalition resisted the threatened use of a dissolution of Parliament as an attempt to circumvent the rights of a parliamentary majority. When the dissolution came, in March 1784, they deplored it as dangerous tampering with the general practise of the past 70 years, which allowed Parliaments to remain in being for almost the whole of the septennial term.[6]

To the King, of course, it all looked very different, 'whether a desperate faction shall not reduce the sovereign to a mere tool in its hands'. To avoid this he, very naturally, was prepared to resort to any device which was not demonstrably unconstitutional. Yet if he regarded the leaders of the Coalition merely as desperate office seekers then he was mistaken. It was the terms upon which they had insisted as a condition for taking office which poisoned the political climate. They were not prepared again to share power with a favourite of the King's choice. Once in office, they intended to conduct government independently of the monarch. No wonder, then, that the constitutional crisis of 1782–4 required for its resolution an appeal to the political nation, for the political situation had reached such an *impasse* that the politicians were powerless to resolve it.

The general election of 1784 was a (fairly predictable) calamity for the opposition. Numerically, it reduced their following from 210–20 to

[6] The Triennial Act of 1694 had declared that General Elections must be held at least every three years. The Septennial Act of 1716 had extended the maximum period between elections to seven years.

130-40. The election aroused opinion and polarized political activity between, on the one hand, those who supported George III and William Pitt and their belief in monarchical independence and, on the other, those who supported the Coalition and its commitment to party government, to the defence of the rights of the Commons and to the limitation of royal power. In this sense, the constitutional struggles of 1782-4 not only defined but also strengthened and enlarged the claims and pretensions of party men. In 1782 the House of Commons could go so far as to remove a ministry appointed by the King. By 1784 the rights of a party in Parliament had expanded, in the opinion of party men, to include the power to determine the composition of the succeeding administration. In the same way, by 1784 a resolution of the House of Commons alone was deemed sufficient by Fox to veto a dissolution of Parliament desired by the monarch, a significant extension of the Coalition's attempt to limit the royal prerogative. Superimposed, therefore, upon the party ideals of the Rockingham Whigs were the political claims fashioned by Fox, Portland and North in the great crisis of 1782-4.[7]

During these years of crisis, the Coalition's fight to survive, its need to unite its forces and to make an effective appeal to public opinion led it to place its proceedings upon a more streamlined organizational basis. The first need was for a steady supply of money. Since the early 1780s a 'general fund' had been in existence which made payments to newspapers and to individuals working for the party. The general election of 1784, especially the Westminster contest, made severe demands upon the fund but its usefulness could not be denied. The heavy expenses attending the Westminster by-election of 1788 led to the opening of a second fund in 1789. Later in the same year, yet a third fund was opened to prepare for the expected general election. These funds were subscribed by party sympathizers, especially the party aristocracy, but the smaller contributions of humbler men should not be discounted. This centralization of party finance was in the hands of William Adam, a Scottish MP and former Northite, who had become close to Fox after 1782. One of the first important party managers in modern British history, Adam would almost certainly have received the Secretaryship of the Treasury in a Whig administration after 1784. Adam had a clear idea of the future of the Whig party. He believed that in recent decades the funded, trading and commercial interests in the Commons had come to challenge the traditional supremacy of the

---

[7] One authority has gone so far as to claim of George III that 'in pursuing his anti-party crusade, his supporters had been forced to adopt the techniques of party itself – letters of attendance, pairing arrangements, co-ordinated tactics, organized propaganda, and electoral planning.' J.A.C. Cannon, *The Fox–North Coalition: Crisis of the Constitution, 1782–84* (CUP, 1969), pp. 235–6.

landed interest. If these rising interests were not to become amenable to royal influence then it was urgently necessary for the Whig party to make a political appeal to them. Consequently, Adam's work for the Whig party went far beyond the raising of party subscriptions. How he spent the money thus assiduously raised is of the first importance.

From his party offices Adam began to make preparations for the general election of 1790 several years beforehand. The weakness of the Whig party in Scotland, for example, he hoped to remedy through his carefully prepared tables of voters and lists of patrons. For England and Wales Adam worked tirelessly, establishing interest in constituencies, cultivating promising contacts and bringing together candidates and constituencies. Small financial payments did a little to ease the problems of local party supporters. He also took pains to cultivate the provincial as well as the London press. By the end of the 1780s most of the London press received money from either government or opposition. By 1790 the opposition controlled five London papers, themselves the key to influencing the provincial press. Adam's central party organization thus became a clearing house for information, money and men, all of which might help the party's fortunes. On occasion, he even sent out party agents to provide specialized assistance. Party organization on this scale and with such ambition and even, at times, sophistication, is a development of considerable significance. The Whig party was subsuming its differences under a party organization which was making a continuous and systematic appeal for extra-parliamentary support.

At the same time, there are clear signs that the party's parliamentary proceedings were acquiring greater order and cohesion. During parliamentary sessions Adam acted as his party's whip, issuing advice on attendance and, on important occasions, sending out attendance notes. He received instructions from opposition peers on the use of their proxies and was informed of the – still traditionally private – pairing arrangements in the Lower House. He was regarded by the government whips, and even by Pitt, as the opposition whip and negotiations concerning the order of business in the Commons seem to have been dealt with by him.

This 'institutionalization' of the opposition unquestionably related to wider developments in British society, notably the rising strength and significance of extra-parliamentary and, especially, provincial opinion, and a growing awareness of the uses to which it might be put. This opinion was now an active political force. Perhaps Pitt had been its first idol in the late 1750s and Bute its first scapegoat. Wilkes had done much to organize it through the power of the press and the parliamentary politicans were ready to court it. Through the press and through petitions Grenville was unsettled, Grafton removed and

North weakened. Before – and after – the election of 1784 Pitt and Fox strove to make effective use of opinion out of doors.

At the same time, the bitterness of the political conflict of 1782–4 imposed upon the Rockinghamite traditions of party co-operation and voluntary cohesion a firmer mould of political organization. This derived partly from the urgent need of the opposition to strengthen itself during these critical years and partly from its somewhat unwieldy coalition structure. The achievement of the party managers of the 1780s, therefore, was to consolidate the Coalition into a party, to absorb smaller opposition factions and, between the elections of 1784 and 1790, to stabilize the size of the parliamentary opposition at around 130–40 MPs.

It would be unwise, however, to underestimate the strength of traditional political forces and influences that still survived in opposition politics. In most places, the customary powers of patrons continued unchallenged and uninterrupted and, in almost all cases, the party machine of Adam had to work through – never against – them. In at least one half of the 83 constituencies in which Adam is known to have intervened an opposition MP already occupied the seat. The party's activities seem, therefore, to have been directed at defending the seats it occupied rather than at launching offensives into hitherto alien territory. Its activities, while significant and interesting, were rarely decisive. Usually, the party's assistance was confined to the writing of letters and the despatch of money. Furthermore, it is difficult to argue that its new bureaucratic machinery did more than allow the party to defend itself. Taking the most generous estimate, the party just about held its own at the general election of 1790. No massive advance was forthcoming. Almost certainly, none was intended.

Notwithstanding their organizational innovations, the Whigs in other respects conformed to the normal pattern of eighteenth-century oppositions. Carelessness and lack of preparation lent a casual and improvised air to their parliamentary tactics. Attendance on most issues was poor and the lead given by Fox was sometimes irresponsible. No doubt these were difficult years for an opposition but for many of their failings the Whigs were themselves responsible. At the root of their demoralization lay the realization that they could expect nothing in the lifetime of the present King. Consequently, they turned their thoughts to his successor and sought to ingratiate themselves with him, thus ensuring their future political prospects. The Prince of Wales, the future George IV, was nothing short of a disaster for the opposition. He used them for his own purposes – usually as a lever to extort more money from Pitt and George III – and cared as little for the real interests of the Whig party as they cared for his. He was an unpopular figure and their identification with him did the Whigs no good at all.

Furthermore, his standing among the party leadership was resented and disliked in many quarters. Burke, for example, never trusted him. Even worse, Fox was unable to stop the Prince's marriage to Mrs Fitzherbert in 1785. The marriage threatened the legitimacy of the opposition for it violated the Royal Marriages Act of 1772 (which required the consent of a monarch to the marriage of a royal) and the Act of Settlement of 1701 (Mrs Fitzherbert was a Catholic). Although Fox denied the growing rumours about the marriage the whole affair was sordid, intensifying the unpopularity and notoriety of the opposition and doing absolutely nothing to convince a sceptical public that they were responsible politicians.

Indeed, the party leadership was seriously deficient in these years. Fox's talents – especially his oratorical abilities – were, of course, absolutely indispensable to his party. The magnetic attraction of his personality and the notoriety of his public conduct gave him matchless influence within his party but he lacked the application, the consistency and, perhaps, the confidence to attempt to transform its fortunes. Nevertheless, by the end of 1780s, there are references to Fox as 'Leader of the Opposition'. The nominal leader of the opposition was, in fact, the Duke of Portland. He was a well-meaning and much respected leader but he lacked political ability and found it difficult to initiate action. Neither man was capable of disciplining the rising, younger men in the party, such as Sheridan and Grey. As for Burke, in the years after Rockingham's death, the great ideologue of party drifted away from a position of central influence. After 1784 he became weary of party and condemned to futility its feeble endeavours. He began to preoccupy himself with the great moral crusade to secure a reformation in the government of India. His attempt to impeach Warren Hastings aroused some excitement within the opposition but long before the end of the decade the party leaders were tiring of the laborious business. The party activities of the Rockingham Whigs had been marked by an exaggerated self-righteousness and a lofty political tone. Such qualities were in short supply in the years after Rockingham's death. Fox might attempt to take party advantage of the Hastings impeachment and rush to replace Pitt when the illness of George III in the winter of 1788–9 promised a Regency, but such tactics were opportunistic. They depended for their success upon the actions of others and upon conditions over which Fox could have little or no control. He thus failed to capitalize upon the organizational developments pioneered by Adam and Portland.

Such scant attention to ideological consistency has led some historians to wonder in what, if any, sense, the opposition Whigs subscribed to common principles, especially when on several of the newer issues of the day, on parliamentary reform, the Abolition of the Slave

Trade, the Repeal of the Test and Corporation Acts, the party was divided. At the same time, there can be no question that the party, far from being monolithic, included powerful sub-groups or factions, such as those led by North, by the Prince and, after 1790, by Burke. Two things may at once be noted. Occasional divisions of opinion on particular issues, especially moral issues, could be tolerated so long as the party's fundamentals were agreed. Furthermore, the strength of the factions within the Whig party must be questioned. North's men were declining quite rapidly in numbers and usually followed Fox's lead. As for the Prince's group, it must be counted in single figures. The alienation of Burke from the party came to be a critical factor only in the 1790s. Before the French Revolution enabled him to restore his reputation, it was not much lamented and in no sense can he be seen as the exponent of an alternative brand of party politics.

The old issues which had sustained the Rockingham Whigs before 1782 were no doubt passing by 1790 but to the Whigs the central issue of the reign of George III was still that of the influence of the Crown. To them the plan of the court remained what it had always been: to destroy the Whig aristocracy and to elevate the prerogative. To the Whigs the King's notorious intervention in the House of Lords in December 1783 had served as a timely reminder that secret influence remained as great a threat to the independence of Parliament as it had been in the 1760s. When a ministerialist sneered at the opposition in 1786 as 'the advocates of the supremacy of the responsibility of the ministers here and for the whole empire' his jibe was enormously significant. The hand of Rockingham thus hung heavy over the Whig party in the 1780s. There may be some rhetorical force in the contention that the Portland Whigs lived in the past. But what parties do not?

Furthermore, it was not merely to the old Rockinghamites that these arguments appealed but to the newer groups, and especially the stream of clever young men who trickled into the party in the 1780s, who learned at Fox's feet to fear the influence of the Crown and who were to spend the rest of their lives fighting it. They would not have done so if they had merely been fed a diet of the stale charges of the age of Bute. Criticism of secret influence gave way to tirades against an overweening First Minister. Fantasies about Bute were transformed into a sincere concern for the independence of Parliament. Consequently, the Whigs condemned bitterly the 'Doctrine of Confidence', by which Pitt claimed the trust of the Commons as a reason for refusing to disclose documents or information. No doubt the opposition after 1784 wore its ideological heart less openly upon its sleeve than the Rockinghams had done. But it would have been surprising indeed if the events of 1782–4 had done other than confirm the suspicions of the previous 20 years. As late as June 1790 *The Times* reported that although the Whigs 'may differ on the ideas of French liberty, their unanimity in the great cause still remains fixed to its final purpose'.

We should not exaggerate the influence of these party ideas. They appealed, at most, to one third of the House of Commons. The rest deplored an exclusive spirit of party. In spite of a superficial political duality, suggested by the conflict between Pitt and Fox, Parliament was not divided into parties. Pitt's ministry rested upon the allegedly uncultivated support of the 'Independent' members as well as that of the Court and Administration group. Pitt abhorred party and governed in the national interest. Indeed, on many issues, such as his reforms of taxation and tariffs and his economical reform measures, there was a substantial measure of agreement between himself and Fox. Consequently, most issues and most parliamentary time had little to do with party politics. It would be difficult to argue that the opposition had an alternative 'programme of measures'. What separated them from Pitt was their past history, their political sympathies and their constitutional instincts. Had they come to office they would have confronted George III with disagreeably novel claims concerning cabinet government and the elimination of royal interference but they would not necessarily have pursued a specific series of measures, except perhaps on the affairs of India and of Ireland, whose governments they wished to change and to reform by weakening royal influence.

In the longer term, Party had come far since Burke's theoretical vindication of 1770. Party government was now the major threat to the monarchy of George III. The battle for the legitimacy of party had been won, in spite of the political reverse suffered in 1783–4. Indeed, the circumstances of that reverse had revivified the relevance of the myth of secret influence. In spite of the manifest failings of the Whig opposition little, if any, of the steady consolidation of party into the routine of politics was lost.

Whatever cohesion the party was able to maintain, however, was gradually weakened and finally destroyed in the conflict of ideas provoked by the French Revolution after 1789. It is tempting to interpret these divisions as the natural consequence of pre-existing differences in the party and to present the ultimate disruption of the Whig party in 1794 as the natural culmination of a long period of disintegration. Such temptations should be resisted. For example, some of the most serious fissures had concerned the affairs of the Prince of Wales but these were much *less* significant after 1790 than they had been earlier. Some historians have been tempted to seek a 'radical' versus 'conservative' axis, equating those who supported Parliamentary reform in the 1780s with the future 'Radical' Foxite Whigs. But half of Fox's men did not support parliamentary reform in 1793. Furthermore, the most critical, single agency of division, the Association of the Friends of the People, a parliamentary reform pressure group formed in the spring of 1792, was more a consequence of the rising political excitement of its time than the natural consequence of earlier developments. It is important to be clear why the Whig party divided. It was over a totally unprecedented issue. Was Britain in the early 1790s in greater danger from popular unrest, as first Burke, and then other sections of the party, including Portland, believed or, as Fox always claimed, from ministerial deception, royal power and executive tyranny? Such an issue could not have been anticipated in the 1780s.

More important than any ideological division was the inability of the party leadership to compose personal differences. The party's neglect of Burke was to cost it dear. Few had taken seriously his statesmanlike approach to the Regency Crisis of 1788–9 and his deep concern for the principle of hereditary succession. Burke drew his own conclusions about the party's seriousness of purpose. Similarly, Fox's reluctance to impose his discipline upon Sheridan and Grey during the Regency Crisis was to bear bitter fruit for the party in the heady days after the French Revolution had inspired such men with dreams of reform which Fox could neither satisfy nor contain.

The first important public split in the party was provoked by the publication of Edmund Burke's *Reflections on the Revolution in France* in November 1790. His passionately reasoned denunciation of the French Revolution was intended to challenge what he considered the dangerous degree of support and respectability which the public statements of Sheridan were lending the Revolution and, more directly, Fox's somewhat casual acceptance of Sheridan's enthusiastic support for the Revolution. Fox disowned Burke and his challenge to his leadership of the party in the summer of 1791. He asserted that the French were imitating the Glorious Revolution. Since the Rockingham party had dedicated itself to the defence of the Whig principles established at the Revolution, it was hardly consistent, he claimed, to desert those principles now. At first, Fox's repudiation of Burke's apocalyptic utterances about the Revolution was generally accepted within the Whig party, although with a few instances of private concern about the direction in which he appeared to be leading the party. Nevertheless, his insistence on the need for party unity, especially at a time when Pitt's foreign policy appeared to be on the verge of provoking a war with Russia, made sense. Such an uneasy compromise could, however, only be maintained so long as Fox's presentation of the Revolution as a 'Whiggish' event could be sustained and so long as he could maintain some control over those in the party whose enthusiasm for the Revolution was leading them to advocate reform at home.

With the formation of the Association of the Friends of the People in April 1792 Fox lost control over the reformers in his party. The Association was an attempt to commit the party to parliamentary reform. At once, a wide section of opinion in the party was worried lest Fox allow the party to become dominated by those who wished it to become a vehicle for securing radical constitutional change. Burke had warned in the *Reflections* of the dangers of well-meaning reforms leading to revolution and chaos. Although Fox did not join the Association he did not disavow its objectives. On the issue of reform at home, therefore, the party had become deeply divided, owing to the precipitate action of the Associators. Fairly or not, Fox became increasingly identified with the reformers in the public mind. As the year advanced, the struggle for Fox's conscience intensified. William Pitt was not above tempting some of the conservative aristocrats in the party with offers of place but as long as Fox might be won back to respectable opinions there was no final split in the party. In December 1792 Pitt issued a Proclamation calling out the militia on the grounds of alleged insurrection. This convinced Fox that Pitt was not to be trusted, that he was out to break the Whig party and to destroy liberal sentiment in the country. He was thus driven into a defence both of the French Revolution and of reform at home. In the Parliamentary debates of the same month Fox ceased to trim. Only his continuing, indeed increasingly intimate, friendship with Portland, together with Portland's mistrust of Pitt, prevented a total split. Even so, early in the new year about 30 MPs deserted Fox and Portland and declared their support for the Government. The first stage of Whig division had thus been accomplished. Although it was not until May 1793 that Fox publicly supported parliamentary reform in the Commons, by then the issue of reform had fatally damaged the unity of the Whig party. It is, of course, true that parliamentary reform had been an 'open' question for many years and that different opinions had long prevailed. But now the circumstances had changed. The issue of reform was so urgent that divergent opinions on its merits could no longer be tolerated.

Even more fatal to party unity were the differences over the war against France. Continuing to believe that the threat from revolutionary France was less dangerous than that from a tyrannical minister and monarch at home, Fox opposed British involvement in the war which broke out against France in February 1793. To demand peace with a regicide republic which was proclaiming revolution throughout Europe was, to say the least, a provocative and unpopular step for Fox to take. Fox did not attempt to defend the excesses of the Revolution but 'Anarchy, if it could be introduced into other nations, was in its nature, temporary – Despotism, we knew, by sad experience, to be lasting.' On such issues there could be no compromise, no trimming. All that could be hoped was that the war would be mercifully short, allowing the Whig party to reunite its divided forces when these great issues could be forgotten. But the war was to last for over 20 years. By the end of 1793 it was becoming clear that earlier expectations of a swift and decisive victory had been dashed. Thereupon, Portland and the conservative Whigs severed their political links with Fox. It was only a matter of time before they formed a Coalition with Pitt, and this they did in July 1794.

The disruption of the Whig party under the impact of the French Revolution cannot be dismissed as an instance of the fragility of party. After all, it required historical events of unprecedented magnitude to force a realignment (not a destruction) of party loyalties. It was, indeed, solicitousness for the soul of the party which motivated Burke in his propaganda, Fox in his attempts to satisfy all men and Portland and the other conservative Whigs in going to almost any lengths to preserve their faith in Fox for so long. It was, in the long run, a reluctant recognition of the impossibility of compromise which made possible the final schism in the party. Yet the habits of party co-operation which had grown up in recent decades were not lightly abandoned. Even when they steeled themselves to join Pitt, the conservative Whigs were determined to carry the principles of the Whig party into the ministry with them – in particular with the intention of reforming the government of Ireland. The Coalition would thus not extinguish party but bring party men into the ministry to enable them to protect the constitution throughout the Empire. The Coalition of the Portland Whigs with Pitt may have divided the *Whig* party, but it did little in the short term to weaken party feeling. When members of the Whig party came to deal with Pitt, there could be no avoiding the recollection of the manner in which he had replaced them in December 1783 and how he had clung to office until the general election of the following year. There was much for Whig souls to brood upon in the memory of these events.

As for Fox, his hatred of Pitt, his untrustworthiness and his double dealing, knew no bounds. For many years, he continued to preach that the country stood in more danger from the King and Pitt than from the forces of the French Revolution. For Fox, 1783 was more important than 1789. To have serious negotiations with Pitt, and to take office in his ministry, was tantamount to conceding the legitimacy of what had happened in the former year. The Coalition of 1794 and the series of events that led up to it, therefore, amount both to a realignment of party loyalties and a reaffirmation of the strength of party in politics. The path to Coalition was a struggle less for office than for the soul of the Whig party and a battle for its future. In the end, it was Fox who emerged victorious. It was he and his followers who, in the event, won the battle for consistency and carried forward the mantle of party, and of Whiggism, into the nineteenth century.

The Foxite Whigs: 1794–1812

For 10 years the Foxite Whigs stood alone in systematic opposition to the war-time ministries of Pitt the Younger and his successor. They could not defeat the minister and could do little more than place on record their opposition to his measures while attempting to carry their case to the public. The public, however, remained sceptical. Its mood was patriotic and it had little time for a party which was advocating peace with the national enemy. The Foxites had, perforce, to fight once again the struggle for the legitimacy of party.

Fox was determined that the Portland–Pitt coalition of July 1794 should not be the end of the Whig party but a new beginning. He saw clearly what the role of party must be in the new political world after 1794. If the war were successful then the executive would receive greater moral and material resources than ever before and liberties might consequently be threatened. By the same token, if the war went badly, then the rights of Englishmen might still be seriously curtailed and rights of assembly and free speech eroded. For Fox, party was 'by far the best system, if not the only one, for supporting the cause of liberty in this country' in such a cruel dilemma. The struggle against the influence of the Crown could only be waged on a party basis. In opposition, the Foxite party would vigorously defend the constitution. This they were capable of doing because as an aristocratic party – and Fox was no less insistent than Burke upon the aristocratic nature of the Whig party – they possessed the tradition of Whig constitutionalism and the independent fortunes needed to resist the blandishments of the court.

In power they would make drastic changes. Not only Pitt but all his associates would be removed and censured. Furthermore, Fox advocated

> Religious liberty to its utmost extent, Reform in Parliament, liberty of the press and indemnity to others (radicals), not only peace but a good understanding with Bonaparte.

This almost amounted to a revolution in church, state and foreign policy. No doubt the luxury of opposition allowed Fox to formulate a lavish theoretical plan of radical change. What is significant, however, is the general support for Fox's objectives in his party. Although, even now, Fox shrank from a general demand to appoint to the entire administration,[8] his brutal frankness does not seem to have worsened the prospects of his party, which survived the 1790s, that most unfavourable of all decades for an opposition party.

This, in itself, was something of an achievement. Indeed, the Foxites seemed to flourish rather well in adversity. As the party emerged from the great upheaval of 1792–4 a parliamentary membership of around 60 can be detected. Thereafter, the frequency with which Fox divided the House of Commons on matters of civil liberty confirmed and may even have enlarged his party's membership. At the general election of 1796 the Foxites maintained their numbers. By 1801 there were 80–90 Foxite Whigs. Although they were both by birth, and, on the admission of their own principles, an essentially aristocratic rather than a popular party, they were much more closely united than either their Portland or Rockinghamite predecessors. Fox stamped his own personality upon his party and welded it tightly together. Familial and ideological sub-groups were much less important in the opposition in the 1790s than they had been in earlier decades.[9] About one-third of its members had been in the Rockingham party before 1780, about one-half had fought Pitt in 1783–4. Whatever their political and ideological experiences were to be in the 1790s, the Foxite Whigs were, at heart, anti-Chathamite, burning with resentment at their treatment at the hands of Pitt and the King in 1782–4.

Consequently, Fox did not abruptly abandon the traditional language of opposition politics. He continued to maintain that the objective of a party in opposition was to obtain office in order to reduce the influence of the Crown. But he went further in asserting his belief in the essential value of the freedom of the individual as the goal of political action. It was this commitment to liberty which gave Foxite Whiggism its distinctive character. Further, Fox was convinced not merely of the desirability of party and of opposition but of the *permanence* of both as a guarantee of the liberty which he so greatly prized. This was giving party a place in the political system of the country which Burke had never envisaged.

---

[8] At about the same time, Charles Grey defined his own conditions for taking office. These included 'a certain indication to the Public that the Government is to be conducted on different principles from those which have prevailed of late years. This can only be done in one of two ways. Either by the adoption of some great and leading measures which would speak for themselves; or by the admission into the Administration of such a number and description of Persons on our side, as, combined with the removal of those whose conduct has been the most obnoxious on the other, would give us a sufficient influence over the general measures of Government, and offer an unequivocal proof of a change of system.'

[9] Towards the end of the decade the Whigs resumed their reversionary interest in the heir apparent. On this occasion, however, they managed to avoid becoming as closely embroiled in his affairs as they had previously, although the Prince's following of 20 MPs and 20 peers considerably strengthened the party's resources.

Foxite Whiggism, consequently, was more than a defensive reaction to the policies of the Younger Pitt and his government. It was further characterized by a positive commitment to the virtues of parliamentary reform. This, of course, flowed from the activities of the Association of the Friends of the People in 1792. At that time, Fox's response had been distinctly lukewarm on account of his anxiety to preserve party unity. In May 1793, however, when Charles Grey proposed the reform of parliament to a sceptical House of Commons, Fox unequivocally supported him and declared his belief in the proposition that the constitution could only be rescued from secret influence by the reform of parliament. This was a bold lead for Fox to give. Only one-third of the members of his party were Associators and only one-half supported him in the division lobby. In 1797 almost all of them did. In May of that year Grey moved for triennial parliaments, the abolition of rotten boroughs, single-member constituencies in the counties and a uniform, rate-paying franchise in the drastically remodelled boroughs. Grey and his colleagues attempted to organize reform committees, modelled on that of Middlesex, to hold meetings and to raise petitions in support of his plan. These endeavours floundered in the face of an indifferent, even hostile, public opinion. The failure of these initiatives should not conceal the courage and energy which went into them, especially in the year of invasion scares, mutinies and witch-hunts against reformers in the country at large.

The Foxites had, in fact, been rather more successful in carrying an appeal to the people some years earlier. They had hastily thrown together an Association which organized public meetings to promote petitions against the 'Gag Acts' in 1795–6.[10] These Acts threatened the existence of the radical societies which had sprung up during the early 1790s under the inspiration of the French Revolution. Most of them were harmless and contented themselves with peacefully seeking the reform of parliament. Ninety-four petitions signed by 130,000 people were raised against the Acts, most of them organized by the popular societies in co-operation with the Friends of the People and the Whig Clubs. Only 30,000 people signed the 65 petitions supporting the Acts. This was impressive enough but the whole campaign, like many before and after, was fatally flawed by the inability of petitions to overturn a ministry supported by a Commons majority. By the end of 1796 the brief alliance between Foxite Whigs and radicals had ended in failure and mutual disillusion. The 'Gag Acts' succeeded in intimidating the radicals, although Fox exaggerated when he spoke of

[10] In October 1795 the King's carriage was attacked by rioters in the streets of London. The ministry responded by rushing through Parliament the Seditious Meetings Bill, whereby the death penalty could be imposed for attendance at unofficial meetings of over 50 persons, and the Treasonable Practices Bill, which made it high treason to speak or write against the constitution.

the 'Euthanasia' which descended upon the country.

The determination of the Foxites to uphold liberty and to advance the cause of reform flowed naturally from their perception of the revolution in France. Having initially welcomed the revolution and having gone so far as to suffer the dissolution of the Old Whig party in defence of the principles of liberty, Fox could do no other than condemn the war against revolutionary France. Indeed, he had already denounced the Brunswick Manifesto of July 1792 which proclaimed the allied Austro–Prussian war aims to be intervention in the internal affairs of France and the destruction of the revolution. Fox asserted the freedom and independence of nations to choose their own governments, to adopt whatever constitutions they chose and, as Great Britain had done in 1688, to cashier their rulers. Fox denied that any nation had the right to interfere in the affairs of another. In spite of the internal turmoil within France, time was needed for the revolution to establish and thus to vindicate itself. Thereafter, France might peacefully take her place among the nations of Europe.

There can be no gainsaying the lofty moral grandeur of these principles. At the same time, they rest upon a very partial view of what was happening in Europe in the 1790s. Fox saw what he wished to see in the Revolution, attempted to justify its excesses and wilfully ignored the danger which it presented to British security. In truth, Fox little understood the affairs of France and endeavoured somewhat blindly to square the events of the unfolding Revolution with the simplistic admiration with which he had greeted its early stages.

Consequently, Fox opposed the British declaration of war upon France in March 1793. From the beginning of British participation in the war, the Foxites advocated recognition of the regicide republic and negotiations for peace. They denied that the opening of the Scheldt and the wild words of the revolutionaries amounted to a *casus belli*. Only the military incorporation of Holland into France would amount to a threat to British security. They condemned Pitt's government for allying itself with the despotic, military regimes of Europe, and for engaging in counter-revolutionary warfare against a country struggling to recover its liberties. Such warfare would simply drive the French to extremes.

In an attempt, therefore, to force Pitt to negotiate with France the Foxites launched an appeal to the public in 1795. The outcome was disappointing. Only 18 peace petitions were forthcoming. Even more significant, candidates who stood on a peace platform at the 1796 general election did badly.[11] Significantly, the Foxites began to shift the

---

[11] Peace candidates won at Devonshire, Norfolk, London Westminster and Liverpool. They were unsuccessful at Leicester, Worcester, Kent, Bristol, Norwich, St Albans and Hertfordshire.

edge of their attack. Increasingly, they condemned the incompetence, the maladministration and the corruption which accompanied the war-effort. Furthermore, when negotiations at last began in January 1797 Fox manifested an equivocal attitude towards them. He was contemptuous of the rapacity of the British negotiators – had they succeeded Britain would have gained parts of the Spanish and Dutch colonies – but he also blamed the obstinacy of the French Directory. The Foxites were coming to view the expansionist objectives of republican France with no little apprehension. Although Fox at first welcomed Napoleon Bonaparte's accession to power in France and continued to advocate negotiations, he had ceased to advocate peace at any price. By the turn of the century, he had come to recognize that the libertarian ideals of the revolution had gradually decayed into imperialistic and nationalistic objectives.

Long before, this, the Foxites had become weary and demoralized. Not only parliament but also the public had chosen to ignore their warnings about war and peace, reform and liberty. Taking the line most conveniently open to oppositions which found themselves in a hopeless situation, they decided upon a temporary secession from parliament. The overwhelming rejection of Grey's motion for parliamentary reform in May 1797 by 256 to 91 was the occasion for the secession. The real reason ran much deeper. Secession would be a public repudiation of the system of secret influence and repression. Secession would starkly reveal to the public the servility of Parliament. Between 1797 and 1801, then, the Foxite Whigs seceded from parliament, to sit and wait for events to vindicate their political wisdom.

Like so many of their proceedings, the secession was a curious mixture of idealism, expediency and disorganization. Confusion accompanied it from the beginning. No formal decision to secede was ever taken and the secession was never complete. Fox did not object to his followers attending on particular issues. His generosity outran his sagacity for if the secession were breached then it lost its point. Nor was the party united on secession. A few, led by George Tierney, and supported by R.B. Sheridan and Philip Francis, continued their parliamentary attendance. Others including Charles Grey quickly came to see that secession was a serious tactical misjudgement. By 1800 they had rejoined Tierney on the opposition benches.

There was every reason why they should. The invasion scare of 1797, the Irish insurrection of 1798 and the establishment of Bonaparte's power in France were momentous events which a responsible opposition party could not ignore. When Napoleon made a peace overture in 1800 the Foxites tacitly ended the secession. Although they were criticized by their opponents for deserting their posts, such criticism provided the most significant commentary possible upon the need for an opposition party. Since 1801 no opposition party has seriously attempted a general, parliamentary secession.

The fall of Pitt in 1801 after his inability to carry the King over the question of Catholic Emancipation for Ireland brought the Foxites flooding back to town. Was this wholly unexpected occurrence not a further example of the sinister operation of secret influence? Even the unassailable Pitt, enjoying large majorities in both Houses, was not immune. The Foxites tested their strength against the new administration led by Henry Addington in a State of the Nation debate on 25 March 1801. The opposition outshone and embarrassed the ministers in debate and, although they lost the division by 291 to 105, it was the most heartening minority figure for almost a decade. For the first time in years, Fox's optimism began to revive. He resumed the active leadership of his party, which he had of late left to Charles Grey, the man he was clearly grooming for the succession. The fall of Pitt had introduced a new element of uncertainty into politics and Fox intended to be its beneficiary. What he could not have realized was that the fall of Pitt was to inaugurate a decade of political instability which not only affected the allegiances of the Foxite Whigs but conspired to bring them into office in 1806.

The political stalemate of recent years was thus already dissolving when the Peace of Amiens – approved by the Commons on 3 November 1801 and signed on 27 March 1802 – threw the political scene into confusion. A 'new opposition' emerged led by Lord Grenville, who had been Pitt's Foreign Secretary, and William Windham, one of the most distinguished and talented of Fox's old friends. It was less their numbers – 20–30 votes in the Commons, 12–15 in the Lords – than their talents and reputation which made this 'new opposition' so influential.

It is important to notice that Windham and Lord Spencer and other members of the 'new opposition' had been party men before the junction with Pitt in 1794. In 1802 their hostility to Addington promised to restore them to their original political home. (Fitzwilliam, indeed, had already returned.) Resentful of Pitt's moderate attitude towards Addington's peace policy the 'new opposition' were gradually to break their links with him. Ironically, just at that moment, Fox and his party, desperate to keep Pitt out of office, helped to sustain Addington.[12] Their support of the Peace was less than convincing. They rejoiced that France had successfully resisted allied attempts to impose despotism on her but grumbled that the Peace was too generous.

---

[12] Tierney even persuaded Grey to have soundings with the ministry with a view to a junction between Addington and the 'old opposition'.

Opinion in the country, however, unreservedly supported the peace. Foxite candidates more than held their own at the General Election, which Addington called in June 1802, to add public vindication to parliamentary approval of his peace policy. Although only a few spectacular breakthroughs were registered – at Kent, Norfolk, Hertfordshire and Middlesex – the election did at least indicate the first significant shifting of public opinion towards the Foxites for more than a decade.

Ironically, it was not long before the Foxites abandoned the policy of peace with France which they had advocated since 1792. It was hardly inconsistent of them to support renewed war against a Napoleonic France which seemed manifestly bent on establishing a hegemony in the continent of which the revolutionary governments of the 1790s had barely dreamed. When Napoleon annexed Piedmont and invaded Switzerland late in 1802 France was now herself violating the principles of non-intervention which Fox had enunciated in the 1790s. Fox ultimately supported the declaration of war upon France in May 1803. The consequence of his action was to be his coalition with Grenville in the following year.

There was a growing body of influential opinion in Fox's party – most prominently the Prince of Wales's group – which strongly supported a war policy and, to this end, co-operation with other political groups. One alternative was to negotiate a coalition with the Addington ministry in order to strengthen its resolve. Addington would not hear of it. The only other alternative was to establish some sort of understanding with the 'new opposition', which just at that time was severing its remaining links with Pitt. It was not particularly surprising that their common views on the need for war against Napoleon would lead to an understanding between the Foxites and the 'new opposition'. What few people expected was the coalition between Fox and Grenville which was negotiated in 1804.

Publicly, it was announced that their understanding amounted to nothing more than a working arrangement between two like-minded opposition groups. Privately, they agreed on a policy of co-operation which extended to the overthrow of Addington and his replacement by a joint ministry formed by themselves. There can be no denying the sheer calculated opportunism of Fox in throwing his fortunes in with those of Grenville. His decision can only be seen as part of a final bid for political power for himself and his party. Still it appeared factious and inconsistent for Fox to throw in his lot with a man whose politics, both domestic and foreign, he had denounced for about fifteen years.

In Fox's defence, it can be urged that his opinions on the war by now converged with those of Grenville: both seem to have been seriously concerned at Addington's ineffective prosecution of the war. On a second major issue, that of Catholic Emancipation, they were also in agreement. Questions of parliamentary reform and civil liberties were, by some contrivance of tacit consent, in a state of abeyance. When they revived, after the war, Foxites and Grenvillites honourably went their separate ways. Furthermore, on economic matters, Fox and Grenville adopted similar views.[13] On most questions, therefore, there was nothing to prevent a coalition. It can be argued that few, if any, of the party fundamentals of the Foxites were endangered by such an agreement. Fox always maintained that Grenville had the makings of a good party man. Like Rockingham and Portland before him, Fox did not object to coalescing with his *quondam* enemies when it was in the interests of his party to do so. There was ample precedent for the coalition of 1804. In any case, what was the alternative? What point was there in a period of further fruitless opposition? Virtue might be preserved but power would never be attained. Furthermore, the 'new opposition' in the Lords included more old Portland Whigs than Grenvilles and there was a smattering of old party men among their number in the Commons. Now that Pitt had acquiesced in a cowardly peace and Fox had come to terms with the war, the coalition was a natural stepping stone on the road to office. As Fox remarked in December 1804; 'Opposition seems now restored, at least to what it was before the Duke of Portland's desertion.'

And yet, such arguments are plausible rationalizations of Fox's ambitious gamble, and nothing more. Whatever apologies can be made for the coalition, there could be no escaping the fact that – and this was the heart of the matter – the Grenvilles were a reactionary gang. They had not only opposed parliamentary reform. They had been deeply implicated in that systematic assault upon popular liberties which had been the very *raison d'être* of Foxite Whiggism. The coalition may have won weight and respectability for the Foxites but it brought them very little parliamentary support. The deal compared very badly with the massive support the Fox–North coalition had brought with it in 1783, when over 100 MPs had come over. Even worse, it caused trouble within Fox's party. Lauderdale and – after some initial enthusiasm – Grey disliked the arrangement, refusing to believe that the Grenvilles were motivated by anything more than sheer malice against Addington. Similarly, the Prince of Wales's group disliked the Grenvilles. Just as serious were the effects upon the public reputation of Fox and his party. The coalition confirmed a

[13] Since May 1803, in fact, the Grenvilles had supported Fox's demand for a committee to examine the financial state of the country. In December 1803 he delivered a stinging condemnation of government's policy of allowing the amount of paper money in existence to increase.

general impression of ruthlessness and inconsistency on Fox's part. In radical circles, Fox's stock fell. The 'Man of the People' of the mid 1790s had first abandoned the struggle for the people's rights during the secession and seemed now to be plotting for his own advancement with men who had threatened the liberties of the country. It was a charge which embarrassed Fox and one which could not be lightly shrugged off.

When Addington's fragile ministry at last expired in May 1804, moreover, it was not Fox and Grenville but Pitt who succeeded him.[14] Pitt in fact persuaded the King to take Grenville but without his new ally Grenville would not serve. Pitt, in fact, proposed Fox but George III refused to have him. Some leading Whigs were thankful that these negotiations failed. Grey, for one, hated the prospect of office and could not bear the idea of seeing Sheridan, now in high favour at Carlton House, in a public and responsible situation.

In the short term then Fox's bid had failed. Nevertheless, the political confusion of the previous three years ensured that the structure of politics during Pitt's second ministry would be very different from that of his first. The comfortable government majorities of Pitt's great years had melted away since 1801. Pitt knew it. He could command the loyalty of the 80 or so Court and Administration Members. Of the rest of the House, he could rely on the personal loyalty of no more than 60 MPs. Addington had about the same number. Fox and Grenville together commanded the votes of about 140. To these could be added up to 30 or so supporters of the Prince.

As was so often the case, weakness in administration was matched by disunity in opposition. The Grenvilles, of course, did not share the simmering resentment of the Foxites against the Pittite system and it took time for the two sides of the Coalition to learn to work together. The Grenvilles could never really understand the personal bitterness which motivated the old opposition. Consequently Fox enjoyed the reconciliation between Pitt and Addington in December 1804 on the grounds that it threatened Pitt's reputation and popularity, not least with his own supporters, while demonstrating to Pitt his own inability to stand alone. The Grenvilles were reluctant to be drawn into a systematic opposition and only unwillingly attended the Prince of Wales's magnificent dinners for the opposition at Carlton House. In 1805 it was with great unhappiness that they joined the Foxite attempt to impeach Henry Dundas (Lord Melville), the First Lord of the Admiralty.[15] A Foxite vote of censure on 8 April was supported by only

---

[14] It is interesting that Addington resigned with a clear, although diminishing, majority in the Commons in order to save the King from being 'forced'. At the same time, Pitt made it quite clear that he would not impose conditions on the monarch.

[15] In February the Tenth Report of the Commissioners of Naval Enquiry found Dundas guilty of financial irregularities during Pitt's first administration.

one-half of the Grenvilles in the Commons. Had the rest followed suit there would have been no need for Speaker Abbot's agonizing and protracted decision to resolve the 216–216 stalemate by casting his vote against Dundas and for almost certain impeachment.

The war caused even more substantial tensions for a time. Fox demanded peace with Napoleon and condemned the timing of the current continental campaign. Grenville, however, supported the campaign and would not near of negotiations. The overwhelming French victory at Austerlitz on 6 January 1806 left Prussia and Austria at Napoleon's mercy. It was now more urgent than ever for Britain to prosecute the war vigorously and Fox was prepared to recognize the fact. Events on the continent and the final collapse of Pitt's administration following his death on 23 January 1806 thus consolidated the Fox–Grenville coalition.

During the final months of Pitt's ministry, in fact, the coalition performed quite effectively. In debate they outshone Pitt's mediocre team in both houses. There was, moreover, a more active air about them. In the 1805 session the House was divided with great regularity. Fox was so confident of the unity of the opposition that he even had the temerity to run his men hard in support of the petition of the Irish Catholics, a surprising gesture in the direction of religious toleration which astounded contemporaries and offended the Prince of Wales. The Melville impeachment, with its unpleasant connotations of corruption, did much to discredit Pitt in his last years and, correspondingly, revived Foxite morale both within and without Parliament. Numerous meetings and petitions supported the opposition and left no doubt where public feeling lay over the Melville scandal. Whatever the judgement on the Fox–Grenville coalition, there can be little doubt that these years witness the revitalization of the Foxite Whigs and the re-establishment for the first time since 1791 of a substantial opposition group in Parliament.

The resignation of the Pittites after Pitt's death left George III no alternative but to turn to Grenville and, with reluctance ('I understand it to be so'), to Fox. The 'Ministry of All the Talents', as its name indicates, was never intended to be a party administration, but an attempt to erect some edifice of stable government in a world of fluctuating groups. Fox had abandoned any notion of a party administration and now his ambition drove him to seek office on almost any terms available, short of conciliating the Pittites. Fox agreed to the inclusion of Sidmouth and his group in the new ministry, at the cost of much personal popularity since Sidmouth's inclusion appeared to rule out the possibility of doing anything for Ireland. At the same time, the somewhat distasteful rush for places and the bitter quarrels between Foxites and Grenvilles over them did little for the new ministry's reputation.[16]

Even worse were the contradictions and inconsistencies which discredited the leaders of the 'Talents' administration. Differences about war and peace surfaced at once, Grenville advocating all-out war, Fox wishing at least to attempt to negotiate with Napoleon. After six months of argument, Fox persuaded the cabinet and the King to allow him to try. This was to be Fox's intended legacy to posterity after the final destruction of Pitt's policies at Austerlitz. In Fox's splendid vision, an era of peace would render possible an era of reform. These noble endeavours sadly failed. His peace policy died with him on 13 September 1806. Grenville seized control and prosecuted an active war policy but with little more success than his predecessors. The 'Talents' ended up fighting Prussia, who had accepted Hanover from Napoleon and Turkey, on behalf of the Russians. To put it mildly, the ministry injected little noticeable new spirit or direction to the war and implemented no reforms of significance.

Rather more blatant – and, in the long run, more damaging – was the ministry's refusal even to entertain a discussion of parliamentary reform. There were, no doubt, many good tactical reasons for that refusal, the hostility of both Houses of Parliament, for one thing, the implacable opposition of the King, for another. What far outweighed these considerations was the public feeling of resentment against the Foxites for repudiating their principles. Fox's refusal to do anything to satisfy reawakening radical demands led, indirectly, but swiftly, to the emergence of an independent radical movement which called down a plague on Whig as well as Tory houses. But what, more than anything else, disgusted the political world and discredited the Whig party was its refusal in office to do anything at all about the evil against which it had been clamouring for decades in opposition, secret influence. The ministers fell over themselves in their efforts to woo the King.[17] Nor did they forget the Prince of Wales. So profligate were his requests for places and sinecures and so readily were they complied with that Pittites began to fear the secret influence of the Prince! Finally, in direct contravention of the Whig notion of the independence of the judiciary, the Lord Chief Justice was brought into the cabinet in an attempt to please Sidmouth and the King. Manifestly, then, the 'Talents' ministry scarcely offered any sort of challenge to secret

[16] If Windham is counted as a Grenvillite and Fitzwilliam as a Foxite the cabinet included five Foxites, three Grenvillites, two attached to Sidmouth and a single adherent of the Prince of Wales, Lord Moira. Lower offices were fairly evenly divided between Foxites and Grenvilles.

[17] Increased provision was obtained for his younger sons and, more surprisingly, the number of Hanoverian troops in England was increased. The Foxites had formerly treated the presence of the King's electoral armies as a dangerous threat to freedom.

influence. The fact was that political union could only be bought at the price of political inconsistency, a price that was ultimately to be paid in the low public opinion of the ministry.

In spite of these harsh realities, the ministry completed the great work of the abolition of the Slave Trade and attempted to do something for Ireland. The Chancellor of the Exchequer, Lord Henry Petty, was closely associated with Wilberforce and the government assumed responsibility for the abolition, both Fox and Grenville honourably fulfilling their earlier obligations to the movement. Although Windham opposed the measure, as he always had done, it gave the ministry an issue to unite around, albeit a non-party issue. On Ireland, the 'Talents' were planning a thorough reform of the system of tithe.[18] Ireland was, therefore, not to be neglected but time was needed to lay the ground for reform. The 'Talents' attempted to purchase it by a Bill allowing Catholics to become officers in the army and navy throughout Great Britain and not, as formerly, in Ireland. At the last minute, Sidmouth and the King refused to interpret the concession to extend to staff appointments. The 'Talents' agreed to drop the Bill. They refused, however, to make a written promise that they would never again raise the question. At this, the King dismissed the ministry.

It is important to be clear that the ministry would have collapsed in any case. Had Grenville and Grey attempted to abandon the Bill there would have been fatal resignations. There was a general feeling, however, that what the King had done was both unconstitutional and unprecedented.[19] The myth of secret influence was within days revivified. The King, it was alleged, had been planning to dish the Whigs all along. He had been scouting for future support even before the final days of the ministry, reposing his confidence in men other than his ministers.[20] Why did he not ask the new ministry, led by the Duke of Portland, for similar pledges? As the Whigs brooded on this latest instance of royal treachery they could not even console themselves with the support of public opinion. Both the immediate reaction

[18] Fox has been heavily criticized for failing to make stipulations in favour of the Irish Catholics when the 'Talents' came into office. But it is difficult to see what else he could have done. The King would have been adamantly opposed and so would Parliament. The Catholic petition of 1805 had been lost by 336 to 124 in the Commons and by 178 to 49 in the Lords. And, as the General Election of 1807 was to confirm, public opinion was vehemently anti-Catholic.

[19] That this feeling was widespread was reflected in the division on 10 April 1807 on a Foxite motion which challenged as unconstitutional the practice of demanding pledges from ministers restraining them from advising the King. The Whigs lost by only 258 to 226. Had the Prince of Wales group and Sidmouth's men voted with them, they would surely have won it.

[20] The Duke of Portland advised the King to act firmly, declare his opinion on the Catholic issue, and be assured of support. It was five days later, on 17 March, that the King asked the 'Talents' for the fateful pledge. George III was well aware when he insisted on the pledge that an alternative administration could be constructed.

to the King's action – in the shape of petitions – and the expression of opinion at the General Election of 1807 showed that the King's action was generally approved. Lord William Russell's defeat at Surrey and Sheridan's at Westminster were the most spectacular setbacks. Yet again, the Whigs faced an indefinite period of opposition, this time identified in the public mind as the party favouring the Catholics.[21]

Inevitably, opposition cut a weak and unconvincing figure during the next few years. The occasional defeats suffered by ministers – on Economical Reform and on the Walcheren expedition in the session of 1810, for example – arose from internal revolts among the ministry's supporters rather than from opposition's exertions. On the two great issues of the time, on war and on reform, the Whigs failed to attract increased support inside and outside Parliament. On the war, their opposition seemed ungenerous and sometimes frivolous. During the years of the Peninsular War any opposition to the attempt to resist Napoleonic domination of Europe was doomed to seem factious. Although the opposition did not advocate peace – at least before 1813[22] – its petty running commentary on the war won it little credit. The Whigs were barren of constructive ideas and bereft of real understanding of the geographical and logistical problems faced by ministers and generals. Between 1810 and 1812 they almost reached the point of demanding that the government abandon Spain with their assertions of the inevitability of defeat and economic ruin. Treating the Peninsular War as a party issue, they sometimes seemed to leave reality behind. Charles Fox had for years maintained an alternative foreign policy, however unrealistic – that of peace. The Whigs between 1807 and 1812 did not have an alternative policy at all, except, apparently, to prostrate the country at the feet of Napoleon without actually making peace with him.

On questions of reform, many members tended to rally round the government in the face of the revival of radical agitation after 1807. The Whigs had the worst of both worlds. Because of their own

[21] They continued to further Catholic claims with consistency and regularity, e.g. in 1808 Lord Grenville moved for a Committee on the Catholic Petition of that year. The Whigs also sponsored the idea that the Crown might have a veto over Roman Catholic bishops, thus ensuring the loyalty of the episcopate. However ingenious, the idea did not commend itself to George III and was treated with indifference in Ireland. Nevertheless, this does represent an alternative policy to that of Emancipation, which they well knew was not feasible during the present reign. It was rejected by 281 to 128 in the Commons on 25 May 1808.
[22] At least not officially. There was, in fact, a good deal of support within the party for the traditional Foxite peace policy. In February 1808 Whitbread's motion for peace was lost by 253 to 108, a very creditable division by the standards of the times. The divisions within the opposition on the question of peace should not be discounted. Sheridan and Holland had the most romantic conception of Spanish nationalism and advocated a policy of assistance. On this, as on other such issues, Grenville and Grey were pessimistic and negative.

indolence, combined with fear of upsetting the Grenvilles, the Whigs failed to sponsor schemes of parliamentary reform, thus cutting themselves off from respectable, middle-class reformist sentiment in the country. At the same time, they did just enough to horrify conservative opinion. In March 1809, for example, Whitbread affirmed his party's continued belief in Grey's 1797 reform proposals. The London radicals reacted strongly and defined their own version of parliamentary reform in Burdett's speech in the Commons on 15 June 1809.[23] To historians exercising the benefit of hindsight, the Whigs' schemes fell far short of those of the radicals. In fact, it is difficult to detect much difference between them. It is true that the radicals attempted to put pressure on the Whigs while, for political reasons, the Whigs strove to appear as moderate as possible. Brand's reform motion of 21 May 1810 attracted 115 votes against a majority of 234, an achievement which would have been impossible had he adopted Burdett's more extravagant rhetoric. It was less the differences of ideology than their different political perspectives which separated the Whigs from the radicals. The radicals could afford to pursue their single goal with rhetorical zeal. The Whigs had to look to their parliamentary and public flanks, and, not least, to the Prince of Wales.

It was during these years that the Prince and the party began to drift apart, a factor which was largely to determine the party's history between 1812 and 1830. The watershed appears to have been the 'Talents' ministry. Rightly or wrongly, the Prince bitterly resented what he took to be the ministry's neglect of him. Grenville disliked him and was reluctant to fawn over him. A committee of the 'Talents' cabinet infuriated him when it refused to bear out the accusations he was contemplating bringing against his wife, Caroline. Finally, and perhaps most critically, the death of Fox severed the most important link between Carlton House and the Whig party. After 1807 it is misleading to depict the opposition as having a reversionary interest in the Prince. He was 'ostentatiously neutral' in his politics thereafter, bitterly disliking Grey and openly repudiating the party's commitment to Catholic reform.

There was little prospect, therefore, that the four separate negotiations to bring the opposition into government which were conducted between September 1809 and June 1812 would meet with success. The Whig party had traditionally demanded stringent conditions. These usually amounted to some control over measures, an even greater control over men, especially in the more important offices, some

---

[23] For Grey's proposals see p. 29 above. Burdett's scheme involved single-member constituencies of equal size, returning Members on a taxpayer's franchise at elections held on the same day on a triennial basis. Such a system was intended to destroy landlord and patron control of the electoral system.

declaration that the existing administration was at an end, that it had come to power unconstitutionally and that its foundations were illegitimate. In short, they wanted to take office as a party in a new administration. There was, of course, very little prospect that such conditions could ever be forthcoming. In September 1809, for example, when Portland resigned on account of his own ill-health and the bitter conflicts between Castlereagh and Canning, the Whigs were invited to join in 'an extended and combined administration'. Grey refused to have anything to do with men who, he claimed, had ruined the country in recent years. Grenville was little more enthusiastic, voicing the constitutional ground that 'the circumstances that attended its appointment' prevented him from joining the administration. Most significantly, the party followers approved what their leaders had done.

The second opportunity which the Whig party had of taking office came with the final illness of George III and the establishment of the Regency early in 1811. It was widely expected that the Regent would appoint a new administration from among his Whig defenders.[24] All such expectations were shattered upon the rock of secret influence. The Whigs were determined that rival cabals and cabinets at Carlton House should not contest power and influence with responsible ministers. Consequently, they refused to tolerate Moira's and Sheridan's influence over the Prince in a future ministry. Their conception of party government by now far outran the Prince's more leisurely, traditional conception of the relationship of a party in opposition with the reversionary interest. In the event, the Prince decided not to change his ministry and the discussions lapsed.

Similar themes dominated the third negotiation, that of February 1812. Once again, the Prince's overtures to the Whigs raised their deepest suspicions. As in 1809, they were not being offered control of a new ministry, merely a re-strengthening of the old. Although hints were dropped about Catholic Emancipation, hints by now were not enough. The Whigs refused the Prince's offer because they could not bring themselves to unite with any part of the existing administration and because they differed so entirely as to measures. The implication, of course, was that they should dictate measures themselves. As for Ireland, they demanded freedom to implement immediate measures of reform before they would agree to serve.

The general opinion of historians has been that the Whigs were right to refuse these overtures. Those of May 1812 were very different. The assassination of Spencer Perceval in that month threw the political

---

[24] They had great difficulty agreeing the distribution of offices. The leadership of the future ministry in the Commons was the critical point. Grenville wanted Canning, the Foxites wanted Whitbread. In the end Grenville gave way.

situation into confusion and roused the country gentlemen in Parliament to demand efficient and stable government. By now, Grey and
Grenville were less hostile than they had been towards the Peninsular
War and some accommodation may have been achieved. Yet again,
the stumbling block was the status of the ministry. For what the Whigs
were being offered was not the freedom to conduct a party ministry but
merely four cabinet places out of twelve, with others going to men who
did not share their opinions and who stood close to the Prince. True,
prospects for Catholic Emancipation were held out but no firm
assurances were offered and the Whigs, although there was some
grumbling from the back benches, remained out.[25] As the two leaders
put it, 'It is to the principle of disunion and jealousy that we object.' In
short, they feared a repetition of the calamities of 1782, and 1783 and
1806–7. Indeed, they derived much of their inspiration, indeed much
instruction, from past events. The lesson they had learned was that it
was too dangerous to join with other groups in office and trust to the
goodwill of a King or a Regent for their safety. A stable party ministry
lay in exclusiveness and party domination of the executive and these
they were by now determined to establish as conditions for taking
office. Here is one underlying reason why the Whig party remained in
opposition until 1830.

By 1812 the Whig party was set in the mould cast between 1782–4,
itself the consequence of political divisions reaching back to the 1760s.
Its proceedings, especially between 1794 and 1797 and between 1809
and 1812, were characterized by a self-conscious consistency, a
neurotic fear of the court – and by now a deep suspicion of executive
power. Yet the Whig party, despite the coalition with Grenville, was
beginning to proceed further and to evolve the beginnings of a programme of progressive reform. Even in the grim, wartime years of the
early nineteenth century they fostered a concern for Ireland, a concern
which embraced both social as well as political aspects, at much
political cost to themselves. Parliamentary reform was a hesitant commitment and a very faint thread but it was just perceptible.[26] Nevertheless, it remains true that what distinguished Foxite Whigs from
supporters of government was, even now, less a polarity between

[25] Grey and Grenville have been much criticized, even ridiculed, for failing to accept
this offer to take office. More particularly, they are excoriated for having made so much
of the Prince's refusal to agree to their demands about the personnel in his household.
But, the attack on secret influence had to begin somewhere and the household was the
obvious place to start to root it out. Their demand for control over the household, therefore, was by no means the insignificant, office-seeking ploy too often described but a
perfectly natural and predictable reflection of their fear of secret influence.

[26] For further discussion of the Whig party's attitude to parliamentary reform, see
below pp. 101–2.

reform and reaction than differing attitudes towards the constitution. The factional politics of the years after 1801 inhibited the germination of the liberal seeds which Fox and others had planted. But time was to show that they would grow and mature.

2 The Rehabilitation of Toryism: 1790–1812

Toryism in the Late Eighteenth Century

While the Whig party was developing – albeit intermittently – in opposition to the ministry of the Younger Pitt, a complex interaction of social and political changes was paving the way for the re-establishment of a new Tory party. The old Tory party of the Stuart period had by stages disappeared during the eighteenth century. Nevertheless, it was a long time dying. Although Walpole had carried out a thorough-going purge of Tories from offices in central and local government, he never succeeded in destroying the old Tory party. Over 100 Tory MPs continued to sit at Westminster, many of them representing populous urban constituencies. It is a serious underestimation of eighteenth-century Toryism to dismiss its representatives as backwoods country gentlemen. Furthermore, Walpole was notably unsuccessful in destroying Tory pretensions. Continuing to regard themselves as the vehicles of an alternative set of principles and objectives, they still believed themselves capable of forming a government, even if this would require alliance with opposition Whigs. Their proscription from office itself imparted a sense of identity which helped to preserve Tory traditions. The jingoism of 'Church and King' together with the popular patriotism of the time could readily become potent rallying cries against a régime which did not stand very high in popular esteem. In the last analysis, Whig leaders of the age might succeed in depriving the Tories of their offices but in an age of proprietorial electoral politics it was altogether impossible to destroy their electoral foundations.

There can be no escaping the fact, however, that by the middle years of the eighteenth century the Tories had failed to sustain their position as an alternative party of government. There are signs that the texture of the party at Westminster was beginning to relax. Its leadership had become weak, divided and indolent. But the Tories were destroyed not by hostile action against them but by the ending of the proscription which had in many ways amounted to their *raison d'etre*. First the elder Pitt and then George III, seeing in the Tories counterweights to the old corps Whigs, ended their proscription. The unity of the old Tories was broken and, effectively, the Tory party may be said to have ceased to exist by the early 1760s.

In the confused and factional politics of that decade Tories are to be found on all sides of the political fence: some supported Bute, others Grenville, others Pitt and some even supported Rockingham's Whigs. Nevertheless, and most significantly, the bulk of them supported the court. In the various 'States of the House' drawn up in the 1760s and on the critical issues separating out supporters from opponents of the court three or even four times as many old Tories supported the court as opposed it. This is not, of course, to argue that the Tory party in any sense survived as a coherent body. But a Tory tradition lingered. Whether the tendency of the Tories to rally round the court amounts to the survival of an old tradition of authoritarianism or the beginnings of a new authoritarian tradition is a nice point. What really matters is the dramatic readiness of the Tory country gentlemen to support the court and, in particular, its American policy. Particularly noteworthy in this respect is the rebellion of many Tories against Rockingham's Repeal of the Stamp Act in 1766 and the absence of opposition from them to North's policy between 1774 and 1776.

> By the 1770s the surviving element in Tory thinking was not the divine right of the monarch, but rather the divine right of properly constituted authority and the non-resistance which certainly lingered on in their political vocabulary was owed not to the King but to the King in Parliament.[1]

Most symbolically, the coercion of America proceeded just at the time when the country gentry were returning to their natural positions in the Commissions of the Peace and in the Militia. That harmony of interest between the court, the government and the country gentry, which achieved its culmination under Pitt the Younger, may already be seen in embryo during the years of the American Revolution. The 'conservative reaction' in British society which historians usually attribute to the 1790s was, in reality, under way earlier. During the 1780s, for example, it received a religious emphasis. It was not difficult for Anglican propagandists to arouse widespread fears and alarms at the repeated attempts to repeal the Test and Corporation Acts in 1787, 1789 and 1790. Fears for the Anglican Church were matched by fears for the Crown. The Regency Crisis of 1788–9 was a distasteful affair which almost saddled the country with a discredited Regent with seriously restricted powers. It did not need the French Revolution to

---

[1] P. Langford, 'Old Whigs, Old Tories and the American Revolution' in *The British Atlantic Empire before the American Revolution*, eds. P. Marshall and G. Williams (1980), p. 124.

teach British public opinion the value of its Church and of its King.

There can be no serious doubt, however, that the French Revolution provoked a vigorous debate in Britain between those already suspicious of reform and those captivated by the libertarian principles of the French Revolution. The writings of Burke together with the dislike felt by the middling and landed orders for the anti-religious drift of the Revolution after the Civil Constitution of the Clergy of July 1790 turned British opinion against reform. As the Revolution proceeded and as radical groups in Britain emerged, ostensibly dedicated to its emulation, then more generalized fears for the preservation of peace and order and the safety of property became widespread. When the violent phase of the French Revolution arrived in the summer of 1792 British public opinion became genuinely alarmed. But it was less the September Massacres than the imprisonment and subsequent execution of Louis XVI which impressed British opinion more than anything had done since the execution of Charles I. It is difficult to overestimate the impact which this highly symbolic attack upon the hereditary principle made upon British political culture. The earlier, more generous sympathy for the Revolution was stifled by a xenophobic reaction against French influences. Once war broke out in February 1793 the prospects for reform had been thoroughly vitiated.

The most potent vehicles of anti-revolutionary sentiment were the Loyal Associations or Reeves Societies, established during the winter of 1792–3 in the wake of the fear of both French invasion and domestic insurrection. When to these threats were added the dangers of economic hardship among the lower orders then the propertied, and especially the landed classes, with the connivance, knowledge and financial encouragement of the government, launched the Associations for the Preservation of Liberty and Property. This 'Association Movement' was an organized campaign against the twin threats of foreign invasion and radical egalitarianism. The Associations distributed cheap or free propaganda of a populist 'Church and King' variety and organized vigilante groups to undertake witch-hunts against radical meeting places, radical publications and radical traders and craftsmen. Local conflict was particularly venemous in communities with histories of religious animosity between Anglican and Dissenter – a significant link with the religious and political conflict of an earlier generation. The country was deluged with a flood of loyalist literature, slogans, songs and rituals. Radicals were harried from pillar to post. In some places they were even forced to conform to the Loyalist platitudes of the day and to join the Loyalist Associations. That profound gulf in the public mentality between conservative and reformer, which was to become one of the most important aspects of British society in the nineteenth century, was beginning. Nevertheless, the Associations (at one time 2,000 of them) created a jingoistic, popular brand of Anglican–Toryism to which many millions of people readily subscribed. Propertied men, especially those from the middling orders, abandoned reform in the wake of one of the most effective processes of politicization in British history. While the upper crust formed anti-Jacobin clubs, taking up such slogans as 'Church and King' or 'King, Lords and Commons' the lower classes burned effigies of Paine.

Although few of the loyalist Associations remained in existence for more than a year, we should not underestimate their lasting achievement in effecting informal, as well as formal, methods of judicial, religious and political control over millions of people. Even then the process of politicization was not complete. It acquired a physical aspect with the spread of Volunteer companies from 1793 onwards, which combined the functions of guarding the country against foreign invasion with suppressing the circulation of foreign ideas. Although the extent to which a 'party of order' was created in the 1790s can be exaggerated – the local party activity of Foxite Whigs, for example, and the occasional revivals of radicalism in certain areas remind us that reformist opinions could not be entirely eradicated – there can be no mistaking the emergence and widespread acceptance of certain political, social and religious values in the 1790s.

The government of Pitt the Younger also played a role, albeit a subsidiary role, in bringing about this climate of repressive opinion. Nevertheless, the Proclamation of May 1792 against Seditious Meetings and publications set the tone. The State Trials of 1793–4 were intended to set an example and were somewhat crudely imitated in the localities. The Suspension of Habeas Corpus in May 1794 and the Two Acts of 1795 and 1796 continued the formal elimination of organized radicalism. The general acquiescence in this massive demonstration of state power can be explained by the prevailing public mood. The mutinies and the threat of foreign invasion of 1797, the subsequent insurrection in Ireland and the Great Famine of 1799–1800 caused a renewal of such activity. Habeas Corpus was further suspended in 1798 and the Combination Acts were passed in 1799 and 1800. The state had assumed an apparently permanent vigilance.

While the government was pursuing 'Tory' measures in defence of the security of the country and while a jingoistic form of 'Tory' public sentiment was sweeping the country, a recognizably Conservative political philosophy was being articulated by Edmund Burke. In his *Reflections on the Revolution in France* (1790) and in his *Appeal from the New to the Old Whigs* (1791)[2] Burke stated the essentials of what posterity recognizes as the Conservative faith. He was not merely opposing the French Revolution and alerting his countrymen to the dangers from France which he predicted. He was protesting against a particular type of politics and political argument. Burke's counter-revolutionary thought is inspired by a profound detestation of rationalistic philosophy. It is this which lends particular significance to his writings. The radical movements of the later eighteenth century had prompted conservative writers to defend the existing constitution but this they had done on practical grounds, such as the absence or weakness of public demand for radical reform of the constitution, or the impracticality of the particular reform measures proposed. Burke elevated the debate to a different plane. Reacting against many of the current fashions of thought – the philosophical rationalism of the Enlightenment, the romantic sentimentalism of Rousseau and others, and, possibly the utilitarianism of Bentham – Burke sought compelling philosophical justification for the cohesive ties of social order.

Repudiating the radicals' myth of a sublime state of nature, from which men peacefully derive their rights and freedoms, Burke argued that society was a thankful liberation from the anarchy of nature. Man's rights derived not from any mythical contract but from the advantages of living in society. Political rights and obligations were not, therefore, matters of choice; they were determined by the nature of society and of man and, not least, by the religious and moral values of Christianity. Inevitably, therefore, any discussion of political rights involved the history of those rights and the activities of man in society.

Burke argued that practices and institutions had a prescriptive legitimacy i.e. they were justified on the grounds of their existence. Institutions of immemorial age, for example, had acquired a legitimacy from their very age and their ability to adapt and change, as man himself had changed. It was this that Burke contrasted with the radicals' belief in the arbitrary and theoretical virtues of rationalist and utilitarian criteria. Burke looked around him and saw with horror what he took to be the destruction of feudal and Christian Europe at the hands of the forces of reason, revolution and atheism. Arguing for monarchy, for aristocracy, for property and for the existing constitutions in Church and State Burke stood on the side of tradition and pragmatic usage, opposed to rationalist speculation and dangerous experiment with the complexities and delicate balances of human society. The fruits of experience and history must not be sacrificed on the altar of rationalism. Burke allowed change and reform but these had to operate

---

[2] Burke was not, of course, the only 'conservative' theorist of the 1790s. For a sympathetic treatment of such writers see H.T. Dickinson, *Liberty and Property* (1977), pp. 290-318.

within the framework of the existing order and must have as their objectives the safe and gradual restoration of an institution to its original purposes. Thus, even in the 1790s Burke remained a 'liberal' with respect to several current issues: the freeing of Irish trade, the relief of Catholic disabilities and the Polish reformed constitution of 1791. Burke wished thus to conserve the timeless heritage of European civilization from the Jacobins and radicals who wished to destroy it.

Burke's conservatism thus emerges from his conceptions of contract, prescription and the state. It is also powerfully informed by his perception of the corruptibility of man and the frailties of his talents. This practical recognition of man's weaknesses – possibly reinforced by his own experience as a party politician, painfully aware of the limitations of political power – restrained him from offering confident generalizations about man's future capacities.

Burke's Conservatism accordingly possesses a vital moral dimension. He believed that there was a higher moral law which man should observe and which he could not alter. This required man to accept certain basic political values which made possible civilized social existence. Thus Burke thought it a moral imperative for statesmen to maintain social order, to use restraint in their exercise of power and to preserve the timeless heritage of the past. The statesman must employ care and prudence; he must negotiate circumstances to enable the state and society to conserve themselves through peaceful change and gradual adaptation.

In arguing that the state should sponsor moderate reform within a prescriptive framework, as a guarantee of civilized social order, Burke was leaving the way clear for more specifically organic and developmental versions of Conservatism. Burke certainly conceded that states and institutions can and must change but change was not to be directed towards some future ideal but towards a past-directed one. Burke had no ideal conception of a future social order. Indeed, his conception of the state and of society has a certain inertia. He recognized their complexity and delicacy ever more strongly as the French Revolution unfolded. Consequently, he came to fear innovation and by the time of his death in 1797 he had become extraordinarily pessimistic about the ·prospects of conserving the British and European heritage.

Arguably, then, Burke's conservatism does not exhibit the 'organic' element, the idea that society naturally grows and develops like any any other organism. Burke did not view the state as a living thing, and specifically rejected the organic analogy. In this he was unlike nineteenth-century conservative theorists who almost invariably adopted it. It may, therefore, be wise to remember that Burke did not regard himself either as a Conservative or as a Tory. He was a Whig, an ex-Rockingham and ex-Portland Whig. He was, of course, a Whig of a conservative kind and one who repudiated Fox's reformist Whiggism. He wished to conserve a Whig constitution. What separated Burke and Fox were their disagreements about how this could best be done. In the last analysis, then, nineteenth-century Conservatism grew out of the Conservative Whiggery of Burke and the Portland Whigs in the loyalist climate of opinion of the early 1790s. To the Toryism of the earlier eighteenth century it owed relatively little, although certain traditions and continuities of sentiment, of local and family allegiance, may at times be discerned.

This is not to minimize Burke's achievement but to place it in correct perspective. There can be no question that Burke paved the way for later expressions of a more thoroughly Conservative philosophy. He widened the province of traditional political philosophy by taking up not merely technical and legal questions concerning rights of resistance and the nature of contract but also wider questions to do with society and its preservation, its history and its continuity and to do with man in his social and religious context. His insistence upon the importance of instinct and emotion, custom and habit, in the life of man and of society unquestionably did much to curtail the realm of reason. If his notion of the state and of society lacked a progressive aspect on account of his pessimistic view of human nature, there can be no question that his recognition of the universality of change in human history allowed those who came after him to develop his ideas in a specifically conservative direction.

The currency of Burke's ideas in the 1790s and afterwards should not be underestimated; they amounted to the conventional wisdom of the age. It was not merely that 300,000 copies of the *Reflections* were sold before Burke's death in 1797. Many of his speeches and pamphlets received a comparable degree of recognition. More significant, however, was the extraordinary saturation of the country in Burkean attitudes and values. Burke confirmed the prejudices and framed the assumptions for a generation of the citizens of Great Britain. His ideas, directly and indirectly, entered into circulation through a variety of sources. The Reeves Associations published cheap editions of his works and, more importantly, popularized versions of his arguments. After his death the *Anti-Jacobin* appeared, a magazine dedicated to the struggle against Jacobinism abroad and Foxite Whiggism at home. It was no accident that this journal was both subsidized by the government and encouraged by Pitt himself. Songs, handbills and prints reinforced Burke's message among society at large. Popular patriotism and organized loyalism, stiffened by government repression, were all vindicated and justified by Burkean concepts and arguments. These attitudes amounted – it should be stressed – to something much more than a political crusade. Burke's ideas were part of the defence and confirmation of existing social and religious, as well as political, values which marked British society in the 1790s. However this phenomenon is depicted – as an upsurge of patriotism, as a religious (evangelical) revival, as a crusade in defence of church and king – the historian is tempted to speak the language of party. A government pursuing 'Tory' policies over law and order, enthusiastically sustained by a 'Tory' public opinion may be seen to profess a Burkean set of 'Conservative' values. Yet the political expression of this phenomenon, the emergence of a Tory party, was to be surprisingly confused and, significantly, long-delayed.

Pittites into Tories 1801–12

So long as Pitt the Younger lived, a new Tory party could not be born. For Pitt was a Whig, an Independent Whig, perhaps, one whose Whiggism stood in contradistinction to that of Fox and his party, but a Whig, nonetheless. Like most politicians of his age, Pitt called himself a Whig, revelled in the Whig tradition of the Glorious Revolution and would have steadfastly refused to recognize himself as a Tory.

All the same, Pitt was a Whig of a singular type. Like his father before him, Pitt was prepared to acknowledge his loyalty to 'Chathamite' principles. He repudiated the principle of party connection, believing that government should be formed from the best men of all parties. He denied that the King's hand should ever be forced by exclusive combinations of men and he rested his ministerial authority upon the confident exercise of the royal prerogative. That Pitt remained in office uninterrupted from 1783 to 1801 was no accident and did not simply reflect upon his administrative abilities. His attitude to the monarchy, to government, to party – albeit Whig – was utterly different to that propounded by the men on the opposition benches. Indeed, he had been summoned to office by a monarch desperate to be liberated from the straits of party. This remained the *raison d'etre* of Pitt's entire political career.

Pitt was not sustained in office by a party but by an informal association of 'Court and Administration' supporters, organized by Treasury men and money. He was, however, dependent for his majority on contentious issues upon the uncultivated support of Independent country gentlemen. What maintained the unity of Pitt's administration was not its agreement on party principles but the much less tangible, though no less compelling, appeals of loyalty to the monarch and service to the country. It is true that Portland's coalition with Pitt injected into it for a time one version of 'party principles' – a curious instance of a group of party men attempting to convert a non-party government to its party ideals. Fox remarked that 'our old friends are worse Tories than those whom they have joined'. Within a few years, however, Portland and his colleagues had been absorbed into the Pittite coalition, its party ideals abandoned and its commitment to Ireland exploded amidst the traumas of Fitzwilliam's vice-royalty.[3]

The effectiveness of Pitt's unchallenged political dominance created an impetus which enabled him to attract, by force of sheer administrative ability and political success, the support of large majorities in both houses. His supporters were administrators and patriots rather than party men. When Pitt fell after his disagreement with the King over Catholic Emancipation in 1801, it did not signify the fall of a party. Most of his supporters were more attached to government than they were to him. The establishment of Addington's ministry amounted to little more than a game of political musical chairs in a non-party political establishment.

Nevertheless, it was perhaps to be expected that such a long-lived ministry should establish a certain cohesion and, in time, a character which sharply distinguished its supporters from those of the Foxite opposition. In particular, the years 1794–7 witnessed the appearance of a sharp ideological gulf between government and opposition. It may be the case that hitherto the essential distinctions in politics had arisen from differing perceptions of the royal prerogative and 'secret influence'. By the turn of the century the Pittites and Foxites were not merely separated by such differences[4] – but by a succession of measures ranging from popular liberties, parliamentary reform to Catholic emancipation. Although nothing resembling a government or 'Tory' party was in existence in 1801, politics had acquired a curiously deceptive 'two-party' appearance.

The fall of Pitt in 1801 enabled the political stalemate of earlier years to dissolve. He had entertained some hopes of making the Act of Union[5] an act of reconciliation by allowing Roman Catholics to sit in

---

[3] One of the conditions for the Whig politicians agreeing to the Coalition had been Pitt's promise that the government of Ireland would be reformed by them. Holding Pitt to his promise, they arranged that Fitzwilliam should become Lord Lieutenant of Ireland. In a dramatic and tragic few months during the winter of 1794–5 Fitzwilliam laboured in vain to effect changes in men and measures in Ireland. Lacking the support of his colleagues, his mission failed and he was recalled to England. The incident marked the effective abandonment of the Portland's Whigs' attempts to inject party vigour into Pitt's administration.

[4] These could themselves become open ended. They amounted to real differences of political as well as of constitutional attitude e.g. Since the 1780s the Foxites had consistently criticized what they termed 'the doctrine of confidence', i.e. Pitt's refusal to divulge information or papers on the grounds that the House reposed its confidence securely in his administration. The Foxites frequently argued that this was a violation of the House's trust but Pitt remained unimpressed by their arguments. He certainly treated the Commons with a high-handed disdain but one with which, in the circumstances, he could justify.

[5] The Act of Union of 1800 united the Parliaments of Ireland and England. After the

the Westminster Parliament. The King determined that to permit Catholic Emancipation would violate his coronation oath and Pitt left office, having promised never to revive the measure in his lifetime. The promise was important. Ultimately and indirectly it enabled the Tory party to become, in terms of its public appeal, the No-Popery party. At the same time, the fall of Pitt demonstrated a growing disenchantment between Crown and minister and, on Pitt's part, a certain wearing down of abilities and health. Perhaps, too, the Foxite secession after 1797 had lulled Pitt into a false sense of security. The removal of systematic constitutional opposition left Pitt and the King without effective parliamentary and political enemies. With the removal of the old enemy, Pitt had to face the problem of managing the King directly. He adopted too high-handed an approach to the monarch and suffered the consequence.

The resignation of Pitt, moreover, was the signal for a fragmentation of the coalition which had governed Britain during the 1790s into Pittites, Addingtonians, Grenvilles and Canningites. Habitual Court and Treasury supporters numbered somewhere between 200 and 230. In a House of 658, after the Act of Union had added 100 Irish MPs, this was scarcely enough to secure reliable majorities. After all, the disposition of the Irish MPs was not yet known and the 70–80 Independent MPs in the House were a further source of unpredictability. A stable ministry required the alliance of at least two of the constituent groups of the old Pittite coalition to supplement and lead the forces of the Court and Treasury party. Pitt had about 60 personal followers after his resignation, Addington 30–40, Grenville 20–30 and Canning 10–15. It took eleven years for three, at least, of these four sub-groups to reunite their forces under Lord Liverpool. (Grenville joined the ministry in 1821.)

Pitt had always refused to cultivate a following and never attempted to transform his supporters into a party. In the unstable politics of the early nineteenth century that dim prospect seemed to recede, with the sharpening of personal differences and the emergence of divisive issues. The factions were divided, especially on Abolition – the Addingtonians were against it, the Grenvilles in favour and the Canningites divided – but also, to some extent, on Catholic Emancipation – the Addingtonians were against it, as Perceval's group was to be later, while the Canningites and Grenvillites favoured it. On the whole, however, there was an underlying unity – on Parliamentary

suppression of the Irish rebellion of 1798 it was thought too dangerous for Ireland to maintain the limited degree of independence which it had until then enjoyed. To persuade the managers of the Irish Parliament to acquiesce in their own liquidation a mixture of bribes and promises was employed, including the promise of Catholic Emancipation, i.e. to enable Catholics to sit in Parliament and to hold public office.

Reform, on Law and Order and, in effect, on Catholic Emancipation. But the extent to which these groups had cohered into a party by the coming to power of Liverpool in 1812 needs careful analysis.

The uncongenial experience of opposition between 1801 and 1804 did something to persuade the Pittites to pull together as a team against Addington's ministry. They were, after all, men of business, accustomed to office, whose political traditions were those of the executive departments of state. Canning had some ideas of reuniting, and transforming, Pitt's connection into a larger party by incorporating just those men who had sustained him through years of peace and war, the country gentlemen. The difficulty with all such schemes was that Pitt would not support them. He would not at first countenance outright opposition to Addington's ministry, its policy of peace and then eventual war. Pitt wished to return to office because he had the high-handed belief that he was necessary for the salvation of the country. It was not, however, by organizing a party that he would bring Addington down but by demoralizing him and his supporters by exposing his manifest deficiencies. This he did by complaining of the ministry's neglect of the nation's security on the seas. It took Pitt to exercise this kind of political flamboyance. Canning recognized as much when he confessed to the Commons in December 1802 that the traditional Chathamite nostrum, 'Measures not Men' was no longer enough. He was not advocating bargains and coalitions with which to storm the closet. He simply wanted Pitt to exert and to declare himself when by so doing he would rally a political group large enough to remove Addington. Grenville saw the danger of Pitt's tactics. They might lead to Pitt's eventual isolation. He begged Pitt to consider acting with Fox but he refused. That refusal made possible the Fox–Grenville coalition. Thereupon, Pitt spotted the danger of his position and tried to persuade the King to deal with Grenville and Fox. The King would have none of it. In the event, Pitt came through these problems, ousted Addington and patched a ministry together. Whether such awkward manoeuvres could ever work again, however, might well be doubted.

Pitt's second ministry of 1804–6, however, failed to reunite his old supporters. The Fox–Grenville Coalition deprived him of support from one quarter and he did not enjoy the support of Addington. In truth the ministry stood upon a narrow basis and calls were frequently heard for the reunion of the Pittites. Indeed, in the circumstances of multi-factional politics the cry for union and comprehension was heard on both sides of the House of Commons, a sure sign of the breakdown of political stability. There was even talk of Fox and Pitt reaching an understanding although, almost inevitably, nothing came of the idea.

Significantly, however, such demands for a union of talents ultimately seated Fox in office.

When Pitt died in January 1806, to be replaced by the 'Talents' ministry, his own followers were no nearer being – or intending to be – a party than they had been in 1801. Yet it was not long before the Pittites, regularly assembled at Canning's for political dinners, were wielding their political muscle as a group. On 20 February 1806 they decided *as a group* to support the government so long as the essentials of Pitt's policies were left unchallenged. They would have nothing to do with systematic opposition. Less than a fortnight later they had reacted to the inclusion of Chief Justice Ellenborough in the 'Talents' cabinet by voting *as a body* against it in the Commons. Indeed they proceeded to form a vigorous and lively opposition to the 'Talents'. They did not repudiate the title, 'the opposition', and cheerfully harassed distracted ministers, forcing them into lengthy and sometimes embarrassing confrontations. They were rapidly learning the need for concert and unanimity as they found the apparent stability of the ministry discouraging. Thus they negotiated as a unit rather than as individuals when Grenville sought to strengthen the administration in June 1806. They laid down conditions before they would agree to enter the administration: their demands – the dissolution of the present ministry and explicit royal consent to the negotiations – were unacceptable. They were, however, significant. Pitt would never have approved of such concerted, organized activity. (Indeed, none other than the old Pittite, Lord Grenville himself, refused to negotiate with a group, preferring to detach individuals). Nevertheless, the future for the Pittites began to look bleak. They were accustomed to dominate the political stage. Now they were merely one group among several. They could only survive if they pulled together.

In July 1806 the opposition leaders formally agreed to oppose systematically a ministry which they believed did not enjoy the royal confidence. This was a yet further step along the road to party cohesion but the inhibitions of a generation could not be lightly tossed aside. One of them wrote that the language of party

> is language I do not understand, nor ever shall until we have a head to us as a party, and some distinct intelligible System to act upon as contradistinguished from that of the Government – without this we are no party, and whether we are in a State to form one is very much a subject of Doubt.[6]

There it was in a nutshell. The lack of a leader had hampered their proceedings throughout the period of the 'Talents' ministry. Who was

[6] Long to William Huskisson, 12 January 1807, B.L. Add. MSS 38737 ff. 183–4, Huskisson Papers.

he to be? The obvious candidate, Grenville, had been ensnared by Fox. The only alternative who was acceptable to all was Portland, the alarmist conservative Whig of the 1790s, by now old and ill, but for all that, widely respected.

On this basis they went into the General Election of 1806. They did not fight it on a party ticket and they did not fight it as a party. It gave them, nonetheless, some experience of co-operative, electoral – as opposed to parliamentary – activity. By the meeting of the new Parliament in December 1806, they were determined not only to oppose the 'Talents' ministry systematically but, if possible, to drive it from office. For a while, at least, they had at last found what they had been seeking ever since Pitt's death, a new role and a new *raison d'etre*. When George III came to replace the 'Talents' he found Portland able and willing to bring his troops into the front line. The Pittites returned thankfully to their natural home, in government.

At the General Election of 1807, party names 'Whig' and 'Tory' came back into use. They described specific attitudes to the prerogative – the epithet 'Tory' was used to describe those who supported the King's action in removing the 'Talents' and in permitting such a speedy dissolution of Parliament. This description was clearly attached to 'Mr Pitt's friends'. The name 'Whig' was, of course, applied to those who were the victims of the King's actions. Even more important, Portland's ministry appealed to the public to support the prerogatives of the King and to ensure 'No Popery' in politics. As in 1784, public opinion was squarely behind the ministry. Scores of petitions and loyal addresses left the matter in no doubt. Nor did the results of the election. As in 1784 the defence of the monarchy and the constitution confirmed the position and authority of a ministry of the King's choice. It was the last occasion upon which such a success was to be achieved by Pittite methods.

The constitutional and political changes of 1806–7 were remarkably similar, in fact, to those of 1782–4 in their impact on British politics. They defined and strengthened political alignments and, in so doing, established the framework of politics for something like two decades. The issues of Catholic Emancipation and the King's exercise of his prerogative sharply distinguished Fox's heirs from those of Pitt while giving some point and some definition to the emerging epithet of 'Tory'. The revival of the religious issue, indeed, was a remarkably potent influence in attaching extra-Parliamentary support to the parliamentary groups.

As a consequence of all this, therefore, the Foxites perceived Portland's ministry as an administration established and maintained by royal influence. This the Pittites steadfastly denied, pointing to his comfortable parliamentary majorities. When Portland's age and health required him to be replaced by Spencer Perceval, the Foxites assumed him to be another royal favourite. To the Pittites, however, Perceval had defended the King's independence of action. In this way, political issues were promising to exorcise the ghost of Pitt. Nostalgia for Pitt was all very well but he had been dead for over three years. As Spencer Perceval – himself an Addingtonian rather than a Pittite – declared:

> We are no longer the sole representatives of Mr Pitt. The magic of that name is in a great degree dissolved, and the principle upon which we must rely to keep us together, and to give us the assistance of floating strength, is the public sentiment of loyalty and attachment to the King.[7]

The gradual transition from Pittite to Tory could hardly be better described.

The debates over the establishment of the Regency in 1810–11 went far towards welding together Perceval's parliamentary majority. The closeness of the divisions on the Regency Bill which established the Prince of Wales as Regent[8] familiarized them with the discipline of parliamentary warfare. Perceval and the old Pittites, however, clung to office, only the Canningites and a newer, small group around Wellesley failed to find a place. The assassination of Perceval in May 1812 and his replacement by Lord Liverpool did not alter the structure of political loyalties for Liverpool took over Perceval's team. His administration was a broad-based regime, the core of which were the old Pittites, united upon a basis of loyalty to the monarch, a belief in service to the country and the defence of established institutions in church and state.

By 1812 a broad-based ministry confronted a party opposition. The ministry pursued measures which contemporaries termed 'Tory' although it is doubtful if its supporters would have regarded themselves as party men or their ministry as a party administration. Maintaining the tradition of Pitt, they believed that political loyalties were owed to a monarch rather than to a party. At the same time, they had unquestionably surmounted Pitt's own detestation of organizing a parliamentary following. The essence of political conflict was between government and opposition rather than between Whig and Tory parties, but it would be a mistake to ignore the very real advances which had been made on the government side of the House of

---

[7] A.S. Foord, *His Majesty's Opposition*, p. 439.

[8] Perceval's bill was an imitation of Pitt's Regency Bill of 1788–9. The Restrictions included inhibitions upon the creation of Peers, control of the King's person and appointments to certain offices. These operated for one year. In early 1812 the Regent, to all intents and purposes, wielded the full powers of the monarchy.

Commons in general, and among the Pittites in particular, in the direction of party cohesion. As historians have frequently noted, politicians felt less need for the rhetoric of party in office than they did in opposition. The symbols of monarchy and the gospel of service to the state were lofty aspirations which were enough to motivate men. At the same time, the disciplines of government and the rewards of office acted as the organizational cements for ministerial men. Lacking these advantages, opposition groups naturally needed to lay much more emphasis upon the idea of party to keep men together.

Professor Cannon has remarked that as early as 1783–4

> in pursuing his anti-party crusade, his [George III's] supporters had been forced to adopt the techniques of party itself – letters of attendance, pairing arrangements, co-ordinated tactics, organized propaganda and electoral planning.[9]

There is everything to suggest that such practices, especially as they touched upon planned propaganda and co-ordinated election campaigns, had developed further since that time. However 'Chathamite' Pitt's ministry may have been, George Rose, Secretary to the Treasury, conducted quite sophisticated election campaigns in 1790 and 1796. His activities closely resemble those of William Adam in 1790. It is extremely interesting that, whatever their ideological differences on the subject of party even as late as 1812 – and these cannot be denied – in practice, both government and opposition were doing very much the same things in very much the same way.

Nevertheless, there can be no question that party was much slower to develop on the government side of the House than on the opposition side. This is not to be explained simply by the weighty force of Pittite tradition. There already existed a formal structure of power in the form of the central government, its departments and offices, and traditions of informal allocations to power within it. Governments were not yet inspired by a *party* motivation and did not need to be. There were to hand powerful traditions to which governments could appeal: service to the monarch, patriotism, defence of the country's institutions and the preservation of law and order. These amounted to comprehensive objectives and all-embracing rather than exclusively party goals. First Lords of the Treasury had to gather support for government from all quarters.

It must be stressed that such generous inclusiveness was less a concrete denial of party attributes than a reflection of the precarious nature of government majorities. The allegiance to ministers of well

[9] J. Cannon, *The Fox–North Coalition: Crisis of the Constitution, 1782–84* (Cambridge University Press, 1969), pp. 235–6.

disciplined, politically ambitious and sometimes talented groups could be critical. In the early nineteenth century governments were weak and were defeated on several occasions. One principal reason for the political instability of the 1800s had been the rapid fragmentation of the old Pittite coalition. Correspondingly, one principal reason for the greater stability which was achieved after 1812 was the reconstitution of that same coalition. The process began under Perceval, when Sidmouth came in. Liverpool won the loyalty of Canning and Wellesley and, in 1821, even that of Grenville. The long years of the Liverpool ministry did much to establish habits of regular support and discipline. Loyalty to the ministry, however, was aroused and fostered less through novel institutions of a party character – although their existence has been hitherto neglected – than through the customary attractions of governmental power and patronage.

By the closing years of the Napoleonic war, the Tory watchwords of the 1790s, loyalty to Church and Crown, the defence of the security of the country and the maintenance of law and order had all become platitudes. The events of the Revolutionary and Napoleonic years had infused them with new relevance, however, and any government dedicated to these objectives, especially one which was continuously faced with an opposition which boasted of its pure Whiggism, was likely to find itself tarred with the brush of Toryism. The ethics of executive Toryism, the defence of the country, the landed interest, property, the established church and resistance to radicalism may have been so generalized that they scarcely amounted to a specific party programme. Indeed, the Whigs agreed with much of it. It would be unhistorical to depict the ministries of Pitt and his successors as reactionary governments confronted by a liberal and progressive Whig opposition. Opinions on Parliamentary Reform, Catholic Emancipation and the Slave Trade sometimes cut across political loyalties. At the same time, the government's frequently negative approach to such questions before the mid 1820s, its identification with political reaction and its self-proclaimed purpose of maintaining the country's institutions amounted to an identifiable Tory mentality.

Although government was still the King's government, and although the Caroline affair in 1820 served as a reminder how explosive the royal issue could still become, the Prince Regent and his successor did not intervene as provocatively in politics as George III had done and there was little serious controversy about the power of the monarchy after 1807. By the early nineteenth century, governments had acquired greater coherence and more independence of the monarch. Ministers and officials owed their loyalty to a Pitt or a Liverpool rather than to the person of the monarch. The intimate, at times almost conspiratorial, relationship which Bute, Grafton and North had enjoyed with their monarch was a thing of the past. The rising power of the cabinet had effectively formalized relations between monarch and ministers. When the King was no longer the first of party leaders, a Tory, rather than a King's government could be said to exist.

3 The Party System of the Early Nineteenth Century

The Evolution of the Two-Party System

Towards the end of the Napoleonic War, and in spite of the inhibitions which that great war placed upon the emergence of parties, the outlines of a stable and coherent party system were becoming visible. True, the lingering hostility to party combinations was still an emotional, and even a political, force to be reckoned with. This old-fashioned resentment against party politics was, however, by now confined to Wilberforce, his 'Saints' and a few score old Independents. The real cry against 'party' was, significantly, a protest against government by influence, government which neglected the popular voice or, alternatively against a factious opposition. During the years of war, however, the Whigs had come to accept the need to resist not only Napoleon but also radicalism at home. Minor parties remained a stubborn, and not infrequently an influential, testament to an earlier epoch. Yet how much could the knots of Grenvilles, of Canningites and Wellesleyans achieve alone? Nuisance value and durability they might have but their days were numbered. Monarchs and ministers were soon to recognize that governments were made and unmade by the great parties, as George IV was to make clear to the Grenvilles in 1820. Then, his dissatisfaction with the Liverpool ministry over its handling of the Caroline affair left him, he realized, no alternative other than the Whigs of Grey. It was the fragility of government majorities and the shortage of capable political leaders which lend the minor factions their contemporary significance rather than any political weight of their own. In spite of the damaging and retarding impact which the Revolutionary and Napoleonic period exerted upon the development of party, it survived the political fragmentation of the early nineteenth century. Indeed, and as so frequently was the case, the recurrence of political instability ultimately quickened party developments.

Furthermore, there are signs that long-term political developments were facilitating the growth and permanence of a party system.[1] The

---

[1] By party 'system' I wish to be understood as meaning a political regime in which a

decline in the power of the Crown, initiated by the Economic Reform legislation of 1782, continued by the administrative reforms of Shelburne and Pitt, was compounded by the personal weaknesses of George III and George IV. As long as George III was active then the decline was effectively concealed. After 1812 almost all politicians recognized that royal favour was of less weight than parliamentary and public support in sustaining a ministry. What George III and Pitt had done in 1783–4 could never be repeated. Nevertheless, it is not the case that what the monarchy lost, the House of Commons gained. The real beneficiary of all this was the cabinet, which was now becoming the effective vehicle of executive action. The fact, therefore, that the Whigs were a party in almost permanent opposition should not conceal the irony that history was going very much the way they had demanded ever since Burke's *Thoughts*.

At the same time, the number of uncommitted MPs in the Commons[2] was rapidly declining. As political issues became both more numerous and more divisive, it became harder to identify a natural, patriotic line of conduct. No doubt such men, *prima facie*, tended to support government, and were to do so again, even after 1815, but the pressures to do otherwise were mounting. It is not just that 'Independence' was becoming harder to maintain. The opportunities for public opinion to make itself felt were rapidly increasing in these years. It was particularly vociferous over high government spending and clamoured for a reduction in war-time levels of taxation. We have already had occasion to draw attention to the rash of general elections in the early nineteenth century. More generally, the role of politics and of parliament in the state was changing quite rapidly. With the emergence of a new industrial civilization, the legislative demands made upon the forms of Parliament, to say nothing of petitions and protests, committees and enquiries, rose steeply. The number of entries in the Journals, for example, increased by 350 per cent between 1760 and 1806.

One of the major reasons for this development was an increasingly vociferous public participation in politics. The rapidly expanding circulation of the press signified the growth of a political consciousness which riveted its attention to proceedings in Parliament. No Prime Minister had to endure the spotlight of publicity and the constant searchlight of hostile criticism that Liverpool had to put up with. The stamps on newspapers sold soared from 9 million in 1760 to 39 million

majority party in the Lower House forms the government, although not necessarily exclusively from its own members. In this regime, the government is confronted by an opposition which differs on certain key and fundamental constitutional and/or political questions and which takes active steps to attempt to replace it. Both parties have generally agreed policies to which their members are expected to be positively committed.

[2] For the growth of party in the House of Lords see below pp. 65–6.

in 1837. The political and radical convulsions of the later eighteenth century had attracted petitions which could be numbered in dozens. The Repeal of the Test and Corporation Act in 1824, on the other hand, is said to have attracted around 5,000 petitions while Catholic Emancipation attracted an incredible 20,000. A political nation was coming into existence on a scale and with a speed that was to transform the structure of British politics by 1832. Furthermore, it was an increasingly homogeneous political nation. In the first two decades of the nineteenth century the London press came first to rival, then to dominate, then to dwarf the collective circulation of its provincial rivals. These qualitative changes in the nature of politics and the extent of political participation facilitated the development of a two-party system of politics. This may be seen in the existence of a 'government' and an 'opposition' press in London from the 1780s onwards. (Independence was scarcely more viable in the press than it was in Parliament.) Newspapers were bought, influenced and cajoled into supporting one or the other side in politics. Sometimes editors made their own decisions and chose to identify themselves and their paper with government or opposition. Whatever the precise circumstance, partisanship was coming to dominate an increasingly powerful press.

The emergence of a predominantly two-party political system is reflected in the fact that in the mid eighteenth century less than a quarter of MPs were party men. By 1832 almost all were. The numbers of Rockingham Whigs in the 1760–82 period fluctuated between 50 and 80. After 1784 the Portland Whigs together with North numbered around 140. An estimate of 1806 allowed the Opposition 150 and the Government 180. It is significant that only half of the House of Commons could be allocated between government and oppositon as late as 1805. Within a couple of years, however, the number of party men exceeded that of non-party MPs. An estimate of 1810 put the Opposition at 214 with 53 possibles, the Government, meaning the Court and Administration and career politicians, at only 80 – and, most interestingly, the anti-oppositionists, i.e. Pittites and Addingtonians at 143. Significantly, about 30 MPs could still be allocated to the small parties. These developments reached their culmination during the political stability of the Liverpool administration when the political warfare of government *v.* opposition, Tory *v.* Whig, came to dominate and in a large degree determine the quality of political relationships.

For one thing, the vast majority of MPs offered consistent support to either government or opposition. Table 1 charts this development for the Parliaments of 1812, 1818 and 1820.[3]

[3] A. Mitchell, *The Whigs in Opposition, 1815–30* (Oxford, 1967), p. 66.

Table 1:

Parliament	Government	Government fringe	Waverers	Opposition fringe	Opposition
1812–18	253	78	102	83	149
1818–20	261	80	48	16	171
1820–26	250	99	114	66	154

The consistency in the extent of support for government and opposition is no less striking. No less than 59 per cent of all MPs in the Parliaments of 1812 and 1818 voted with absolute and unvarying consistency. When all three Parliaments are taken together, 51 per cent of all MPs never deviate in their voting behaviour. Most of those who do change their allegiance do so only slightly, e.g. from support of opposition or government to fringe support of opposition or government, and so on.[4] These general figures ranging over entire Parliaments perhaps give a conflated view of what actually happened in a particular session. In the session 1821–2 320 MPs supported the Government, 226 the Opposition, 23 supported both (only 3 per cent) while 89 did not vote at all. In 1823 only 20 MPs voted both ways and only 11 did not vote. Furthermore, 'party' divisions were now quite regularly outnumbering 'non-party' divisions. Quite simply, Parliament was expending a greater proportion of its time debating party issues and dealing with them in a party manner.

It is important to place this trend in a relevant historical perspective. This situation is quite different to that which had prevailed in the 1790s, when Pitt's government had massive majorities as it dwarfed the tiny rump of Foxite Whigs. This situation is also quite different to the confused and fragmented political situation which had prevailed in the first decade of the new century. This can best be illustrated by the formation of the Ministry of All the Talents. In 1806 there were only 150 Foxite Whigs and Grenvilles. They would thus have to work with the 180 or so committed 'Government' MPs if a ministry were to survive in Parliament. This was not enough for a comfortable government majority. Therefore, Fox chose to ally with Sidmouth – he could not possibly have allied with the Pittites – and his 40-odd followers. This is the politics of fragmentation. During Liverpool's ministry, however, a stable government faced a stable opposition party. Of course, it is possible to detect a number of less than enthusiastic followers of both but the politics of party had come to prevail over the politics of independence, of anarchy and of fragmentation. And, it might be added, of neglect and indifference. In the 1790s and early 1800s 200–250 MPs would fail to attend Parliament in a particular

[4] *ibid.*, pp. 253–5.

session. As we have seen, that number had been reduced to well under 100 in the years of Liverpool's ministry. The ideal of committed and expected support for either government or opposition had replaced the mid eighteenth-century ideal of political independence.

We should not imagine that party activity was confined to the House of Commons. Although we should make allowance for the inability of the House of Lords to mount the sort of resistance to royal and ministerial policy of which the lower House was on occasion capable, we should not leave it entirely out of account. It is true that the Peers spent most of their time on the small print of Private and Local bills, on technical rather than on polemical matters. Nevertheless, the upper chamber was not immune from political developments. Although most Peers were not party men at this time – scarcely surprising when politics was not the principal business of their lordships – there are signs that party divisions were beginning to make an indelible appearance among them.

The House of Lords was dominated numerically by a somewhat diffuse group of men who might most conveniently be labelled 'King's Friends'. These were united by loyalty to the Crown and constitution rather than by any political opinions. They were predisposed to support any administration in which the King reposed his confidence but they were not a group organized in its support. They constituted about one half of the Chamber. Next in size were the active politicians. Their numbers were increasing quite rapidly. There were about 50 of them in 1785, over 100 by 1805. Although ministerialists were usually in a comfortable majority, the opposition could occasionally attract one third of this group. Any government was therefore dependent for its security upon the 'King's Friends'. Finally, a small group within the House was manifestly Independent in its behaviour. Such peers numbered 35 in 1785 but had shrunk to 20 in 1805, in some ways a significant decline in the attraction of independency in politics.

The importance of party activity in the upper chamber should not be artificially inflated. It was, in many ways, the shadow not the substance of party conflict. Particular political issues, however, translated the partisanship of the Commons to the Lords, as happened in 1783–4, 1788–9 and 1801, for example. On such occasions, the opposition rarely threatened the ministry either in debate or in the division. Opposition peers were usually no match for the well-briefed and well-prepared ministerialists. The Rockingham and Portland peers were tentatively managed and rarely did more than go through the motions of attacking the government. The Coalition of 1794 deprived the Foxites of over half their peers, including some of the more talented. The attenuated rump of Foxite peers could do little more than provide the formalities of an opposition. With the secession of 1797 even this disappeared.

By the early nineteenth century, however, party divisions had come to stay. Whatever its other consequences, the Fox–Grenville coalition did something to stiffen Foxite resistance in the upper chamber. Grenville himself was a valuable and weighty acquisition, Lord Spencer an experienced lieutenant. By this time both government and opposition peers had developed formal organizations in the upper House. The Earl of Albemarle was the opposition Whip, sending out his appeals to attend on printed forms. Lord Grenville was an effective Leader of the Opposition in the House of Lords, a position which, in spite of Portland's energetic activity in the 1780s, had failed to acquire continuity. On the government side, the Leader of the House was developing and enlarging his authority. In the 1780s he had enjoyed essentially organizational responsibility. By the early nineteenth century he had become the representative and spokesman of the ministry. Effective organization in the Lords had one, often overlooked, advantage. When at least 25 per cent of MPs had patrons in the upper House, to secure the patron was to secure his client. Party in one House implied party in the other.

Indeed, attitudes to party were changing rapidly. The forms and conventions of the House of Commons itself are perhaps the best and most reliable indicator of this shift in attitudes. In the eighteenth century, Parliamentary business had been arranged by the Speaker in consultation with ministers. Now, it was the leaders of Government and Opposition who did so. Further, as more technical and specialized information became necessary for the business of government, the use of select committees increased, their membership significantly reflecting the balance of party forces in the Commons. Parliamentary procedure, which had originally acted as a defence of the rights of the Commons against the pretensions of the Crown, was now exploited by politicians in opposition to protect themselves and what they believed to be the public interest against the pretensions of government. Such activities accustomed not only the Whig opposition but also the public to political and party activity. Parliamentary proceedings were consequently very much open to public view, and susceptible to public opinion.

Although there were few significant changes in the forms of procedure, the ambiguity and flexibility of parliamentary forms permitted growth and development as the temper of the House changed during and after the years of war. In 1811 Mondays and Fridays were established as Order Days, i.e. days in which government business took priority over all other matters. While this restricted the facility of Opposition to bring forward critical business, or 'notices', it did serve to define the order of Parliamentary business. Nevertheless, the Executive was quite unable to dominate Parliament. Governments had to live with it, to persuade it and sometimes suffer themselves to be defeated by it. There was little they could do to force the House of Commons against its will. The Opposition had a string of procedural expedients to hand, especially the threat to move an adjournment motion, to attack ministers, to frighten them and, on occasion, to filli-buster their proceedings.

The language and, indeed, the assumption of politics were by now indicating that a gradual if intermittent transition to a securely based two-party system was under way. One of the preconditions of a two-party system is the general acceptance of the need for opposition. The legitimacy of formed and regular opposition was, in fact, well estab-lished long before the end of the war. It was perhaps less the legitimacy of opposition which inhibited the development of parties than the tactical problems of securing assent and agreement within the Whig party and, to some extent, the natural timidity of opposition politicians to activate a potentially dangerous and angry public opinion during the years of war. Nevertheless, the very weakness of the Foxites rendered the need for an opposition all the more evident. *The Morning Chronicle* of 13 July 1802 yearned for an opposition which would 'approach in strength so near to the power of Government as to be an effectual check upon them . . . an active, honest, constitutional opposition, which should have influence to prevent encroachments on the great charter of our liberties.' Even during the years of war the assumptions prevailed that a responsible opposition was an integral part of the constitution; that ministers should never enjoy too easy a ride; that an occasional reverse acted as a salutary reminder to ministers that ultimate power was not theirs to dispose but lay with Parliament. The justification for opposition was just as relevant after the war with the revival of conten-tious religious and political issues. By this time, political opposition needed no apology.

Opposition was one thing, party quite another. After all, the right to oppose the measures of government, whether those of a King or a cabinet, had a long and venerable history. Party had a far less unimpeachable ancestry and continually needed justification. It is significant, however, that by about 1812 it was being argued that party was essential to the balance of the constitution. By then most observers accepted the legitimacy of party and of party competition, not least because it was a vehicle for securing and structuring public partici-pation in the political system.

Yet for long there remained a considerable reluctance to use party labels and to focus the language of politics exclusively upon party idioms. This may perhaps be accounted for by the prolonged confusion over party ideals. The reluctance of the Whigs to press the issues of Catholic Emancipation and parliamentary reform, the sensible pragmatism of the Pitt ministry and of its successors, the presence on the government side of the House of proponents of Catholic Emancipation and even parliamentary reform did much to confuse ideological polarities. After all, Whigs and Tories alike believed in the virtues of economy and of maintaining a weak central government. Neither believed – and here most radicals agreed with them – that it ought to be the business of government to 'solve' the country's social problems.

The self-conscious Whiggism of the Opposition was even less precisely defined than it might have been because of personal and political failings, on the one hand, and tactical expedients, on the other. As for the government, its Toryism was tempered by the exigencies of power and by the liberalism of some of its most influential members. Huskisson's economic policy, Peel's reform of the criminal law and Canning's foreign policy speak for themselves. Nevertheless, there can be no denying that the distinction between government and opposition was no longer, even as early as 1812, simply between those who deplored party and those who advocated it. By the end of the war, growing programmatic differences were coming to the surface amidst a general and tacit agreement upon the practical necessity for party combination. Although no one can seriously suggest that elections were a judgement on alternative programmes of measures, they were losing their hitherto claustrophobically local character. Even at unexciting elections, such as that of 1802, the press is full of references to national issues, to questions of war and peace, to questions of reform. *The Morning Chronicle* of 30 June 1802 noted that one of the candidates at Sudbury opposed the war. Its report of the Herefordshire County meeting recounted its discussions of the nature of Whiggism. Even at a particularly 'issue-free' election, such as that of 1806, which was not well covered in the press owing to preoccupation with foreign and military affairs, a non-party issue like that of the Slave Trade struck chords in many constituencies. In 1807 the universality of the party issues of royal power, of ministerial relations with the King, of pledges and of Catholic Emancipation demonstrates that partisan issues could be a factor at elections.

It is not merely the general approval of formed opposition, the acceptance of party politics and the emergence of increasingly ideological elements in elections which signal the party politicization of British life. By 1812 both Government and Opposition supporters had made martyrs of Pitt and Fox and, most significantly, launched near-religious cults to preserve their memories and to enhance their reputations. After his death, Fox became a greater influence over his party than he had ever been while he lived. He was depicted as a towering martyr for liberty and his career as an heroic crusade against royal and ministerial corruption. With the benefit of hindsight, the powerful functions of this mythology were to yoke together permanently and glorify two somewhat ambivalent aspects of Whiggism. The first was the traditional eighteenth-century insistence that the Whig constitution of the eighteenth century had been made by the great Revolution families of 1688, that the Whigs were its natural custodians, the Whig families its natural champions and the rising influence of the Crown and of its ministers its natural enemies. The second, deriving chronologically from the first, was that the influence of the Crown and its ministers was a greater danger to British liberties than the French Revolution, or those radical reform groups in England and Scotland which derived their activities from 'Revolution principles'. The libertarian Fox of 1794–7 was thus superimposed upon the Rockingham Whigs of the 1770s.

No less material is the corresponding idealization of Pitt. Soon after his death, Pitt Clubs sprang up in around 40–50 places, to provide concrete testimony to the growing idolization of 'the pilot who weathered the storm', and to cement the nationalist sentiments which had swept the country during the years of war. The cults of Pitt and Fox, the dinners on their anniversaries, together with the rapidly proliferating busts, biographies and pictures of the two men provide a significant commentary on the political consciousness of the parliamentary classes at this time and the extent to which personal, political and even party conflict had become not merely tolerated but even glamourized.

The mordant irony of history ensured that both Pitt and Fox were followed on their respective sides of the House by men of much more limited stature. Portland's age and infirmities restricted his energy and kept his colleagues manoeuvring for the succession. The Duke of Portland, the only man in British history to lead both a 'Whig' administration (that of 1783) and a 'Tory' one (that of 1807–9), had experience and good sense but lacked the force of will and the ability to recreate the Pittite coalition. His successor as First Lord of the Treasury, Spencer Perceval (1809–12) strove gamely to rebuild the wartime coalition as a government of national unity but he failed to gain the support not only of Sidmouth and Canning but also of Grenville and Grey. Not before the ministry of Liverpool was statesman like leadership on the ministerial side of the House to be re-established.

On the opposition side, it took considerably longer. Fox was not succeeded by one leader. He was succeeded by two, Grenville and Grey, the 'Consuls of the Coalition', as G.M. Trevelyan once described them. They were both convinced that the ruin of the country was at hand, and viewed the future with dark foreboding. Grenville's obduracy snuffed out the promising schemes of reform which Whitbread and others were contemplating, an attitude which provoked the disenchantment of the radicals with the opposition. Grey had somewhat more humane instincts although his major attributes were those of rank and dignity. His greatest political asset, his oratorical ability, was utterly wasted after his elevation to the Lords following his father's death in November 1807. With both leaders of the party marooned in the Lords, who would lead it in the Commons? The obvious candidate was Whitebread but Grenville would not have him. In the end, George Ponsonby, an affable but nondescript incompetent was chosen, and he remained leader of the Opposition in the Commons until his death in 1817. The only conceivable alternative, Lord Henry Petty, was, like Grey, removed to the Lords on the death of his father, Lansdowne, in November 1809. Few historians have had a good word to say about Ponsonby but he was honest and did his best for his party. For his weaknesses, the party grandees must be held partly responsible, at least, for they treated him with scant respect. In many ways, Ponsonby was the symptom, not the cause, of Whig failings. It is doubtful if even Fox could have supplied the personal and political initiative which might have rescued his party from opposition after 1807, or even composed its differences. The extent of such afflictions should not be underestimated. So many of the weaknesses of the Whig party in the next 20 years – the apathy, the complacency, the personal recriminations, the indolence and the failure to build a solid, popular base – can be traced to failings of leadership. Charles Fox must have wept in his grave.

In spite, then, of their very differing origins and political styles the ministerial party in the House of Commons resembled the Whig opposition in several significant particulars. Both were unwieldy political forces, difficult to co-ordinate, nightmarish to lead. Parliamentary managers on both sides of both Houses are to be forever heard grumbling at the unreliability of the attendance of their supporters. As the governing party evolved into a Tory party, imperceptibly distancing itself from the monarch, so the Whig opposition was becoming less of a reversionary party. The Prince of Wales was never on the same terms with Fox's successors as he had been with Fox and the failure of the Whigs to take office in 1811–12 sealed their fate. These somewhat looser relationships between parliamentary politicians and members of the royal family may explain the persisting sense of uncertainty exhibited by ministerialists and oppositionists alike as to the extent of their reliable support. One of the traditional disciplines of parliamentary politics was eroding, to be replaced with the ideological and organizational apparatus of party politics.

Party in the Constituencies

Before 1832 the development of party was located primarily within Parliament and parties existed principally within the House of Commons. No examination of party development, however, can be complete which does not move outside Parliament and into the constituencies. To what extent do the emerging distinctions between Whigs and Tories at Westminster reflect similar distinctions in electoral opinion in the constituencies? To what extent, if any, may a dimension of continuity be detected between the Whig and Tory parties of the early eighteenth and early nineteenth centuries in the constituencies? Given the very varied local situations, any answer to such questions must be qualified and tentative, especially in an area of enquiry into which historians have not been fond of straying.

In the English and Welsh counties, the party conflicts of an earlier age had almost entirely expired. The difficulty of contesting county elections, their enormous expense and the inevitable disruption they entailed had curtailed political, to say nothing of party, conflict by the middle of the eighteenth century. In about one half of the counties, the Hanoverian Whigs had established such a domination of local places and powers that the Tories almost disappeared as a force to be reckoned with. Party labels, when they were used, evoked the bitter feuds of an earlier age; they bore little relation to the current realities of Whig dominion. Such electoral conflict as survived in county constituencies lost any significant connection with the party alignments of Westminster. Electoral politics in these places turned upon support for, and correspondingly, opposition to, oligarchic control by certain landed families. More genuine issues might follow from these dynastic and local quarrels and resentments and could assume a quite sophisticated character, evocative of the party activity of later generations. Hampshire, for example, contained a large number of borough constituencies, some of which experienced contested elections with some frequency. Perhaps for this reason, Hampshire was a politically conscious county. This was reflected in the activities of the Hampshire Club, which attracted opposition elements after 1775. Opposing the American War and supporting parliamentary reform, it can only be described as a Foxite agency during the Regency Crisis of 1788–9 and the election of 1790. What is interesting about the Hampshire Club, and indeed, several other local vehicles of party[6] is less their existence and their activity – these cannot be questioned – than their general failure to maintain themselves and to survive. The Hampshire Club,

---

[5] *ibid.*, p. 4.
[6] The Buckinghamshire Independent Club was a Foxite organization, founded in 1784, and survived until about 1810. It impinged mainly upon county politics but had some influence at Wycombe and Aylesbury.

for example, continued its activities in a regular and systematic fashion until 1798, after 4,000 people had attended a peace meeting in the previous year. Thereafter, its activities become more intermittent. They revived in the political crisis of 1806–7, when there existed both a Whig and Tory Club in Hampshire, but thereafter these groups disappeared.

This may, of course, have been exceptional. But it was not uncommon in other places for the renewal of party activity in the constituencies to reflect the alignments of Westminster politics. This is so, for example, in the 1770s in Bedfordshire, Berkshire, and Norfolk, where there existed a strong Rockinghamite presence. It is true also of Surrey, owing to the Rockinghamite affiliations of many Surrey land-owners, and, more clearly, of Kent and of Yorkshire. In such places, county politics and county elections were informed with, although not always dominated by, a perceptible, Whig *v.* Tory, Opposition *v.* Government polarity. A similar pattern may be detected, though rather more faintly, and certainly more intermittently, in Dorset and Suffolk. In still others, notably Middlesex and Hertfordshire, the party distinctions of the early century had not entirely disappeared when the issues of radicalism and America intruded to activate the independence of their electorates. Political issues counted for much in these places. In Hertfordshire, at least, a radical brand of Whiggism ultimately emerged dominant from the cluster of contested elections in 1784, 1790, 1796, 1802 and 1805. A similar pattern may be detected at Middlesex, where a strong Foxite presence, interacting with radical elements, conspired to unsettle the peace of the county after 1780.

In all such cases, the problem is to determine what is typical. It is important, nevertheless, to appreciate what could happen even under the unreformed electoral system. In fact, in about one half of county seats,[7] some evidence of party activity, or of the use of party labels, or of some local identification with parliamentary parties may be discerned before 1832. This is not to deny the essentially *local* inspiration for county contests, merely to affirm the appearance of party elements in these elections. In many of these cases, moreover, it cannot be denied that party activity comes late. In Sussex it appears in 1820. In some others not before the great crises over Catholic Emancipation (Derbyshire is a good example), and Reform (Shropshire in 1831). It is

---

[7] I can detect little if any sign of historically interesting party activity in Cambridge-shire, Cheshire, Huntingdonshire, Herefordshire (?), Lancashire, Nottinghamshire, Rutland, Wiltshire and Worcestershire. While there is a little evidence for the following, I cannot regard it as other than incidental. Cumberland, Northumberland, Westmorland and Durham had their feuds and at times saw the intervention of party men (e.g. Lord Brougham in Westmorland) but the contests are not moderated by party issues. I am similarly sceptical of Northants, Staffordshire, Wiltshire, Cornwall, Gloucestershire and Lincolnshire.

impossible to detect unbroken *continuity* of party activity in most counties. It is, on the other hand, impossible to ignore evidence of accumulating party activity in at least half of them.

Problems of analysis are even greater in the case of the 203 English and 12 Welsh borough constituencies. In about one quarter of them[8] serious political life had disappeared with the imposition of oligarchy in the age of Walpole and the reduction in the size of their electorates. Many of these boroughs, however, had been 'safe' seats even before 1715. Their closing up in the mid-eighteenth century occasions little wonder, and it is surprising that generations of historians have expressed such indignation at the existence of closed boroughs. In a further quarter, while political life of a sort existed it would be stretching credulity too far to relate it to party consciousness. In some of these cases, sheer venality made a mockery of politics. In others, the patrons were so overwhelmingly powerful that what political activity there was represented nothing more complicated than futile and sometimes venally inspired protests against control from above. In about one-half of borough constituencies, however, something of interest to the historian of party may be found.

In some constituencies, there can be little doubt that continuity of party activity had been broken in the mid-eighteenth century, when the earlier party distinctions had been replaced by the conflict between the oligarchy of patrons and the rights of voters and even non-voters to participate in the life of the town. Later on, however, a revival of party nomenclature is unmistakeable. In some places, (e.g. Derby, Newcastle-under-Lyme, Penryn, Peterborough, Stafford, Tamworth, Warwick and Wells) such terminology is almost entirely incidental rather than descriptive; it certainly does not suggest any significant connection between local and parliamentary parties. In other boroughs, however, the revival of party activity is somewhat more significant. In Boston in the 1790s and thereafter regular contests and newly-divisive issues reinforced the earlier conflict between the Whig Bertie family and the Tory corporation. The contest of 1784 at Northampton established the foundations upon which the politics of the town were founded in the next century, where the Spencers can only be regarded as the ancestors of the local Whigs, and the Independents those of the Tories. Flurries of party activity at Beverley, Tewkesbury and Cardiff also seem to have made a lasting impact upon the political life of the town.

There is a further category of seats where the marked political alignments of patrons and proprietors could do no other than import party

---

[8] The Corporation, the smaller and venal burgage boroughs, the smallest Freeman and scot and lot boroughs.

attitudes and party awareness. It includes Hull, Carlisle, Preston, Wigan, and possibly Portsmouth. The otherwise independent seats of Leominster and Chichester could not quite escape from the reverberations of party, probably occasioned by the loyalties of the Dukes of Norfolk and of Richmond respectively. A further (fairly numerous) category of seats includes those which manifest a significant awareness of the distinctions between government and opposition at Westminster. While local issues in these seats no doubt still predominated there can be no gainsaying the persistent agitation of national issues and loyalties. Aylesbury exhibited fairly consistent party divisions. Bridgewater was frequently contested; its candidates and would-be patrons assuming partisan political attitudes towards national issues. Conventry was a large, regularly contesting borough, usually assumed by historians to have been preoccupied with local issues.[9] In fact, its tumultuous politics involved a strong vein of popular Toryism at the end of the eighteenth century which clashed with the Dissenting traditions and sympathies of the town's corporation. Dover, Rochester and Sandwich contested regularly, the local strength of the government and the size of the electorate rendering it impossible to avoid something of a Government *v.* Opposition axis. Durham's conflict between the Lambton and Tempest families maintained partisanship until the Foxite Whiggism of the Lambton family in the 1790s gave a more firmly national orientation to Durham politics. Lichfield showed a rather similar pattern, an enduring two-party polarity maintained by family divisions, refreshed by the issues of the later period. Comparable boroughs, where party may have provided some of the stimulus for local divisions, would possibly include Abingdon, Bedford, Chester, Colchester, Great Yarmouth, Lewes, Lincoln, Maidstone, Newark, New Windsor, Norwich, Reading, Rochester, Southampton, Worcester, and Newcastle-upon-Tyne.

Finally, a number of seats with large electorates enjoyed fairly sophisticated local party organizations and a strong and keen awareness of national issues. In these places, local groups self-consciously identified themselves with the parliamentary parties. These included Bristol, from time to time Liverpool, Exeter, Gloucester, Ipswich, Westminster, and York. It would be impossible to describe the politics of these boroughs without some reference to the framework of national parties by the second decade of the nineteenth century. The politics of these boroughs anticipated the pattern of politics in many boroughs after 1832 in their juxtaposition of political awareness, party organization and party attachments. Party was not the only element. Some of

---

[9] L.B. Namier and J. Brooke, *The House of Commons, 1754–90*, (3 vols. 1964, HMSO), I, pp. 401–2.

these places spawned a local radicalism which not infrequently made some impact upon the national scene. In all of them, of course, local issues continued to count for much. But in all of them, party had come to stay.

We must not exaggerate either the extent or the function of party in the constituencies. We cannot repeat often enough that the stuff of politics in most places was local, political horizons were parochial and political organizations operated with little or no contact with central party machinery. Many politicians donned a party mantle at Westminster but were reluctant to wear it in their constituencies. It was by no means unknown for men of the same party at Westminster to fight each other at elections, although such cases are exceptional. In the eyes of local people to foment party strife was no way for a decent politician to behave. To do so endangered the security and good order of the community and threatened to set family against family. Increasingly, however, party men at Westminster wore their party labels more openly on their sleeves whenever the parliamentary conflict intensified and whenever it was in their interests to appeal for popular support for their party.

Whatever the exact degree of party awareness in the constituencies, there can be no escaping the extraordinary phenomenon, so much neglected by historians, of party voting at elections, i.e. the tendency for the electors to dispose of both of their votes to candidates of the same party. Assuming that the electors were faced with a clear choice between two identifiable political groups, the electorate automatically aligned itself into two disciplined armies of party voters. At four-cornered contests, over 80 per cent of electors voted a clear party ticket, at three-cornered contests about 65 per cent. What is even more spectacular is the loyalty of the voters to their parties. Where there were contests at successive elections, only around 10 per cent would completely switch both their votes from one party to the other.[10] All this is evidence not merely of the massive organizational exertions of local parties but also of the awareness on the part of electors of the tactical possibilities open to them. Voting, in short, was a carefully considered as well as a carefully controlled activity and one which operated within a party framework. What explains these undeniably strong party tendencies within the electorate at a time when parties either did not exist, or were only fitfully coming into existence at Westminster and when they made relatively little attempt to centralize electoral activity?

Conventional explanations would dwell upon material factors such

[10] These comments refer to parliamentary general elections and bye-elections. They apply also to the much less well known phenomenon of municipal elections for mayor, aldermen, sheriff and so on. These were often just as keenly fought by the same local groups as fought parliamentary elections and supported by much the same voters.

as corruption, social factors such as 'influence' and 'patronage' and political factors such as organization. Such elements must be part of the explanation – in some places, no doubt, the whole of the explanation. They· cannot, however, adequately explain the existence of party voting in the larger boroughs, where the effectiveness of such techniques was much less than in constituencies where one family or institution commanded the obedience of the electorate. Even where techniques of persuasion existed – and no one can deny their near-universality – they were frequently combined with appeals to local party sentiment and loyalty. Such appeals to party sentiment are appeals to opinion and possibly to tradition as much as to dynastic and personal loyalty. As such, they should not be underestimated.

What is the historian to make of these party tendencies within the unreformed electorate? As great national parties once more began to dominate politics at Westminster in the early nineteenth century, and as the frequency of general elections began to increase,[11] the parties began to appeal to the constituencies for men and money. There they encountered scores of locally oriented party systems inhabiting a political culture of their own. These local groups were the heirs of the parties of the early eighteenth century and the indelible imprint which they had left upon political consciousness in England. Long after Whig and Tory parties had ceased to exist at the national level, the psychology of party persisted in the constituencies. Even after the great national issues, of the succession, of religion and of foreign policy, had subsided there still remained serious and fundamental questions concerning political participation in the Hanoverian regime.

The Whigs of Walpole's day had consolidated their hold on the country by restricting the size of electorates by statutory and other devices. Although election contests became less frequent and although the purposes of electoral conflict became steadily more parochial as the Tories lost their *raison d'etre*, election issues were still of immediate local significance. Local appeals to party tradition were, not surprisingly, enormously durable. By the middle of the century, and where purely personal and venal influences had not entirely obliterated political action, the abiding political issue in most constituencies arose from the conflict between the forces of oligarchy and restriction of the franchise, on the one hand, and those of 'independence' and extension of the franchise, on the other. These latter sentiments chimed in conveniently with the popular mythology of the Free Born Englishmen. Election conflict, therefore, turned on the attitudes to be adopted towards the local oligarchy, where there was one, and attempts to strengthen or weaken it. Elections thus concern the question of

[11] See above p. ix.

access to local power and patronage and raise the problem of the acquiescence of the community in the local manifestation of Hanoverian oligarchy.

The Foxite press constantly maintained the exaggerated view that the Foxite Whigs represented these (often permanent) local opposition groups. There was sufficient similarity between the unsuccessful plight of local independence groups, woefully striving against local corporations and patrons, and the Foxites woefully struggling against the largest corporation (the government) and the largest patron (the King) of all, for obvious comparisons to be made. The Foxite press took the 'Friends of Liberty' or 'Friends of Independence' to their hearts and carefully noted their progress, quietly ignoring what Foxite patrons were doing to their own independent voters. They perceived themselves and local independence groups to be involved in a common crusade against a common enemy. The fact that the larger and more populous constituencies tended to provide more than their fair share of opposition MPs while the government was supported by well over one half of the MPs for smaller seats gave some superficial justification to this Foxite assumption. However, since any organizational, personal and even ideological link between the Foxites and these local 'independence' groups has yet to be demonstrated, it is dangerous to accept Foxite propaganda at its face value.

When, however, to the perfectly serious and germane issues of constituency politics are added the increasingly frequent appearance of national issues, then the phenomenon of party voting in the constituencies becomes readily understandable. After the emergence of a vibrant public opinion, associated with the person of John Wilkes in the 1760s, further combustible political controversy flared up with the American rebellion and then with the great constitutional crisis of 1782–4, culminating in the General Election of 1784. After the French Revolution, a rapid series of political, constitutional and religious issues accumulated which activated political and party feeling throughout the country. In view of all this, it is surely none too difficult to understand the party dispositions of the electorate.

There may also be a religious as well as a secular explanation for it. At least, the old Whig historians of the last century, now consistently reviled, used to think so and they may well have been right. For politics and religion were almost impossible to separate in this period. It was not just that church and chapel were sources of propaganda and agencies of electoral recruitment. Nor was it merely the fact that in this period, religion comes to play an increasingly important function in education, philanthropy, and the evolution of humanitarian movements in general. Certainly, candidates in many constituencies sought religious as they would have sought secular interests or support. They frequently behaved as though certain local religious groups, especially the Dissenters, voted as a body.

The Old Dissenters, indeed, were a remarkably active group within the electorate. They were, unquestionably, the heir of powerful traditions of political involvement. Although there is no need to subscribe to that idealization of the Dissenters which associates them with almost every humanitarian movement and every liberal endeavour of the period, there can be no doubt that in many places – by no means in all – they were unusually active in politics. Many of them had the vote and most of them had an acute municipal consciousness. In over 30, and possibly even 40, of the most populous and most economically advanced constituencies the Dissenters were a powerful force to be reckoned with. In most of these, and probably in many others, they formed or acted as the leavening for opposition groups. In the following Freeman boroughs, the Dissenters were thus the focus and catalyst for civic oppositions: Exeter, Ipswich, Liverpool, Leicester, Lincoln, Maldon, Cambridge, Great Yarmouth, Carmarthen, Maidstone, Norwich, Worcester, Wycombe. At Colchester, the Dissenters were the largest group *in* the Corporation. In Nottingham and Coventry the Dissenters controlled the Corporation and confronted Anglican oppositions. Even in smaller boroughs, the Dissenters were a force to be reckoned with. In the tiny Corporation boroughs of Buckingham, Harwich and Tiverton, the Dissenters constituted such opposition as there was. In the somewhat larger and less easily controlled Householder boroughs, the Dissenters found a congenial political breeding ground, as at Cirencester, Northampton, Preston and Hertford. Finally, in a handful of smaller scot and lot boroughs, Dissenters provided the core of opposition to established interests: at Abingdon, Aylesbury, Bridport, Bridgwater and Ilchester. Finally, in the two county constituencies of Hertfordshire and Northumberland, the Dissenters supplied invaluable energy for the oppositions. The overwhelming tendency was for Dissenters to unite with other local opposition groups in their struggles against oligarchy. The activities of Dissenters, therefore, conspired to effect the partisan voting behaviour which is such a pronounced feature of the unreformed electorate.

The geographical distribution of these constituencies is most revealing. It cuts two swathes, one from the south west up to the northwest, taking in Taunton, Exeter, Tiverton, Bridport, Ilchester, Bridgwater and Bristol, up through Carmarthen, Cirencester and Worcester to reach Liverpool and Preston. On the other side of the country a group of constituencies around Maldon, Hertford, Hertfordshire, Colchester, Harwich and Cambridge, stretch out to Ipswich, Great Yarmouth and Norwich, then to Nottingham, Leicester and Lincoln.

It is not merely the stability of the geographical distribution of dissenting constituencies which is relevant to the emergence of a two-party system. They span a fairly wide range of constituency types. Not surprisingly, they include a fair representation of commercial and industrial centres in which politics was more 'open' than in the traditional, corporate towns. These centres include Bristol, Coventry, Hertford, Leicester, Northampton, Nottingham and Tiverton. Next there are a group of smaller market towns but which, stood on unusually good lines of communication: Buckingham, Cirencester, Colchester, Lewes, Maidstone, Taunton and Wycombe. We should also notice the heavy representation of the ports, from which ideas and people could and did flow freely: Bridport, Harwich, Ipswich, Liverpool and Portsmouth. Finally we may note the number of cathedral cities where the dominant presence of an Anglican establishment bred a countervailing reaction from local Dissenters. These include Exeter, Lincoln, Norwich and Worcester.

These dissenting constituencies are those which exhibit patterns of advanced political participation. They are also among the first constituencies to embrace party. In Nottingham, for example, there can be no doubt that the leaders of the Dissenters were self-consciously Foxite Whigs. To ignore this is to midunderstand the politics of the town in the later eighteenth and early nineteenth centuries. Fox had actively courted the Dissenters nationally in 1790 and they proceeded to share in his warm acceptance of the French Revolution. As common victims of the loyalist reaction of the 1790s, they recalled with gratitude his endeavours to secure the repeal of the Test and Corporation Acts in the late 1780s. The connections between the Foxite Whigs and the Dissenters should not be exaggerated. In many places the Dissenters were divided among themselves; in others they remained peacefully apolitical. Furthermore, the Dissenters cannot have taken kindly to Foxite sympathy for Catholic Emancipation in the early nineteenth century. Nevertheless, there can be little doubting the contribution which the Dissenters made to the public audience for Foxite Whiggism and, even in local terms, for effecting two-party alignments.

Party in the constituencies rested upon a solid foundation of traditional political, as well as dynamic religious, considerations. Local party warfare was characterized by its increasingly sophisticated organizational apparatus. Few constituencies were without their clubs and societies, their rituals and their calendars of birth-dates, anniversaries and celebrations. These clubs were the local agencies of party organization before central party institutions reached out to touch the constituencies. They were enormously varied. Some had a religious and others even an occupational quality. Some, a minority, used the words 'Whig' and 'Tory'. Others used the seventeenth-century terminology of colours, the Yellows *v*. Blues of Ipswich, for example. Yet others called themselves after the local inn or tavern where they assembled. In yet others, the enigmatic 'Constitutional' club might find itself in conflict with 'The Independent Club'. Such associations are to be found not only in the larger boroughs, where the writ of patrons did not run very strongly. In medium, and even in some small boroughs, such clubs and associations were the mechanisms through which patrons endeavoured to control the voters, and, sometimes through which the voters protected themselves against the patron. Many of them, in fact, began as the offspring of electoral interests. By the early nineteenth century, some were developing a life and a momentum of their own. Although the fine nomenclature of some of them could not hide the close relationship they enjoyed with a local patron or interest, yet others were concerned with perpetuating and widening political divisions in local society. Even before 1832, therefore, in perhaps one half of borough constituencies, but rather fewer county seats, nascent party institutions were playing a prominent and frequently indispensable role in the life of their communities.

In an age which knew nothing of nationally organized political bodies and which looked with considerable scepticism upon any attempts to establish them, it was only natural that political impetus came from the localities rather than from the centre. Historians usually look for early anticipations of later versions of bureaucratic, centralized party. They should not impose anachronistic interpretations upon the facts. Local men and interests, in fact, endeavoured to exploit national bodies – the government, the church, the services, etc. – for local purposes to procure power and patronage. It was upon realities and assumptions such as these that party activity in the constituencies rested. After 1832 the formal links between central party office and local party groups strengthened appreciably. That such links were much more informal – and sometimes less tangible – in the decades before the Reform Act does not render them negligible.

4 Government and Opposition: 1812–27

Party and People: 1812–20

The years of the lengthy administration of Lord Liverpool (1812–27) witness a remarkable consistency of support for government and opposition. The conditions for political stability which we noticed earlier – the acquiescence of the monarch in his ministry, the security of the kingdom and the maintenance of the Protestant constitution – were satisfied. (When, towards the end of the 1820s, this was no longer the case, then political uncertainty returned.) Nevertheless, there were periods when the security of the ministry came under serious challenge. These were years of social and economic dislocation which gave rise to a bitterness in political conflict which had not been seen since the mid 1790s. If *political* stability had been an earlier stimulus to the evolution of parties then the threat of *social* instability, especially in the years 1815–20, fuelled the fires of partisanship between government and opposition to a dangerous extent.

Nevertheless, as we noted earlier, party politics tends to conserve existing institutions. There were large areas of common ground between government and opposition, especially those bearing upon social hierarchy, the protection of property and the preservation of law and order. Even so, the fact that there was a limit to the intensity of the political battle does not imply that it was a phoney war. The unsettled state of the country tempted the opposition to go to the brink of safety, as it roused extra-parliamentary support for its anti-government agitation.

The ability of Liverpool to establish a lasting administration depended only in part upon his success in reconstituting the old Pittite coalition. Although he enjoyed the support of the groups around Sidmouth and the deceased Perceval he was unable to secure those of Canning and Wellesley. His failure to do so, paradoxically, confirmed his position and highlighted the need for loyalty towards himself and his administration. As W.R. Brock wrote 40 years ago: 'The position of Liverpool was made the cardinal point in the composition of a Tory ministry.'[1] The General Election of 1812 strengthened the ministry slightly but, more importantly, it revealed that the attention of the country was concentrated upon the war against Napoleon. Of all the elections of the early nineteenth century that of 1812 is the least fully reported in the press, a reasonable indication of where public concern lay. Wellington's continuing success silenced the critics of the war and Liverpool basked in the reflected glow of his victories.

By the end of 1812 the opposition was cursing its ill fortune. It was not just that the Whigs had failed to establish themselves in office during the political upheavals of 1811–12. They had failed to capitalize on their success in modifying the Orders in Council. These had been Perceval's response to Napoleon's attempt to impose an economic blockade against Britain in 1806–7. The Orders of 1807 strictly regulated Europe's trade with neutrals. The ensuing economic warfare seriously dislocated Britain's trade and industry and caused considerable distress in manufacturing districts. Thanks to the energies of the young and radical Henry Brougham, and his carefully orchestrated nationwide agitation, the government modified the Orders in June 1812. This alliance of the Whig opposition with the middling and lower orders in urban provincial areas was a remarkable anticipation of the pattern of agitation which was to ensure the passage of parliamentary reform in 1831–2. It was, however, disliked by the party leadership and Grey had counselled against it. Furthermore, it bore little fruit at the 1812 election. Brougham, and about 25 others, fought on a peace platform but they were clearly out of tune with the mood of the country and the party failed to increase its numerical support in Parliament. This remained for some years around 150. Indeed, in 1812 Brougham and Tierney and a number of other leading Whig politicians either failed to find a seat or were defeated.

The series of victories which distinguished the British war effort between 1812 and 1815 was enough to discredit such pacificist tendencies. Indeed, the Grenvilles were dedicated to all-out war, except in the peninsula, the destruction of France and the removal of Napoleon. They were closer to the national mood than the Foxites. The heirs of Fox yearned for peace. These differences between the Grenvilles and Grey, who actually began to advocate peace in October 1813, almost broke the coalition. Grey's diplomatic silence – and the fact that Parliament was in recess from December 1813 to March 1814 – helped to preserve it. The coming of peace in 1814 promised to remove these differences but they were thrown into even sharper reality during Napoleon's Hundred Days. The question of peace or

[1] W.R. Brock, *Lord Liverpool and Liberal Toryism* (1941), p. 21.

war was now dramatically focused. The Grenvilles demanded the overthrow of Napoleon. The Foxites advocated the doctrine of non-intervention in the affairs of a country whose enthusiastic reception of Napoleon amounted to a free and popular choice of its ruler. Grey and Grenville cobbled together a somewhat anodyne formula advocating the strengthening of the armed forces and closer co-operation with the allies. It papered over the cracks but it left the opposition helpless observers of the final drama of Waterloo.

Even so, the ending of the war failed to compose these differences. If the Foxites could not stomach a war to remove Napoleon then they could hardly welcome the reimposition of the Bourbons upon the French by an army of occupation. No wonder that the Opposition lacked both policy and plans when the peace treaties were debated in February 1816. Consequently, ministers had the easiest of rides in securing the endorsement of the peace treaties which returned France to the boundaries of 1790 and imposed upon her an army of occupation of 150,000 men.

Gradually, however, with the return of peace, domestic questions came once more to the centre of public concern. The return to a peace-time economy proved to be painful and thus financial and economic issues commanded the attention of politicians in the immediate post-war years. On these, as generations of historians have remarked, there were no dramatic ideological divisions between the government and the opposition. Both wished to protect and to preserve the prevailing structure of power and property; both believed in a *laissez-faire* economy with minimal government intervention; both espoused capitalist individualism rather than the corporate paternalism of an earlier age. Such divisions of opinion as there were – and these should not be underestimated – existed within the government and within the opposition. Consequently Whigs and Tories were fond of complimenting themselves that such questions could be treated without party rancour. The economic policies of the Liverpool govern-ment, whatever their precise inspiration – and some recent historians have begun to challenge the view that the ministry was embarking consciously upon a free-trade excursion – were often too much for its right wing. At the same time, the individualism of men like Horner cut little ice with the great landed magnates of the Whig party. Indeed, after his death in 1817, the Whigs had no effective economic spokes-man in the Commons while in the Lords Lansdowne was closer to Liverpool than he was to Grenville and Grey.

It follows, therefore, that the Corn Law of 1815 betokened the government's response to the most powerful pressure group of the age, the landed interest, rather than a considered manifestation of its 'Tory' beliefs. By the same token, the Whigs did not regard it as a party measure and its landed members were anxious to support it. Others joined Peel and certain sections of the manufacturing interest in opposing it.[2] Similarly, the tedious and technical financial questions surrounding the government's decision to return to the Gold Standard in 1819 were never a clear-cut party affair. They was treated as part of the necessary post-war restructuring of government financing, which indeed they were. To preserve a stable currency in order to safeguard the property of merchants and creditors, with the resultant beneficial effects upon economic stability, prices and employment, was so fundamental an objective that it could scarcely count as a party issue. For this reason, there was little formal opposition to the government's final enactments in 1819, amounting to a plan for a staged return to the Gold Standard between February 1819 and May 1823.

Nevertheless, the government was extremely careful to prevent the opposition from making political capital out of the issue. Common ground on such an issue there inevitably must be but in an age of party such a hallowed plot could easily be violated. Indeed, when the Committee which ultimately recommended the return to payments on a gold basis was being established in January 1819 Liverpool received little thanks for including such a generous proportion of Whigs. Indeed, they responded by challenging the Committee's terms of reference on 26 January. The division figure of 277 to 168 indicates both the ministers' strength and the readiness of the opposition to lapse into partisanship whenever an opportunity presented itself, even upon such customarily non-party issues.

Whig opposition to Liverpool's economic and financial policies was charged more by opportunism and political expediency than by a rival economic theory. In particular, the government was intensely vulnerable in the area of finance. It had to continue into peace-time with war-time levels of taxation if the army of occupation in France were to be paid for, to say nothing of soldiers' pensions, the promised half-pay to soldiers returning from the war and the drastically reduced value of the pound. In the circumstances, the government had no alternative but to continue with the unpopular Property (or, more accurately, Income) Tax. Inevitable this might be but it could be no other than enormously unpopular, especially when it had been universally assumed that the tax would be a temporary war-time measure. When the government's

---

[2] The ending of the Continental System and the excellent harvest of 1813 had resulted in a glut of cheap corn. The bad harvest of 1814 led to a dramatic influx of cheap foreign imports. An all-party Committee of the Commons was set up in 1814 to investigate the state of agriculture and as a result of its deliberations the government enacted a Corn Law a year later which excluded foreign imports until the price of home-grown wheat had reached 80 s per quarter. The Corn Law elicited an instantaneous, and often riotous, attack upon the landed interest and a landed Parliament for a blatant piece of self-interested legislation.

proposal to renew the tax came before the Commons on 18 March 1816, the opposition voted it down – its first important political victory in years – by 238 to 201.

There is little mystery about the reasons for the government's defeat. In spite of substantial concessions (which included a wider range of exemptions from the tax, the reduction in the standard rate from 2 s to 1 s in the £ and the establishment of more confidential procedures for its assessment and collection) the government fell a victim to an outburst of public hostility to the tax. This occurred on a scale which took ministers, blithely assuming a majority of 40 for their proposal, by surprise. About 80 regular supporters of government joined the opposition and almost as many abstained. Hardly any of those who turned against the government on this issue allowed their obduracy to become a habit. They might be willing to fire a warning shot across the bows of the government for persisting with an unpopular tax but it was quite another thing to deprive Liverpool of their confidence and support.

This highlighted the dilemma in which the opposition found themselves. They had persuaded large numbers of MPs to resort to their constitutional Parliamentary duty of refusing to lend indiscriminate support to ministers and, in this case, to refuse supply. They failed to go further. It by no means followed that a revolt against the ministry on the Property Tax amounted to a desire to install Grey and Grenville in office. Indeed, in 1816 the opposition did not even have the government on the run. They had no further successes and the government quietly recovered its composure – and its supporters. It accepted its chastisement with good grace and, perhaps, with a certain resignation. Ministers made little attempt to influence public opinion, to raise petitions or to distribute propaganda. Recognizing that a tidal wave of public opinion was swelling up and threatening to deluge them, the government battened down the hatches and patiently waited to ride out the storm. After the storm had subsided, the political weather continued much as before.

All of this suggests that the opposition was less instrumental in agitating the issue of the Property Tax than has sometimes been suggested. Admittedly, the Whigs were hungry for political success in 1815–16 and were quick to spot the movement of public opinion. (As early as November 1814 they had been laying plans for a campaign against the tax.) But the hostility of the public to the renewal of the tax was not originated by them. It was spontaneously generated in the country once the government's intentions to renew the tax – widely publicized by the opposition – had become known. Although some 400 petitions reached the Commons, almost all of them against the tax, 'There is no evidence of any central planning or co-ordination, nor of any direct stimulus beyond the efforts of individual Whigs in their own localities.'[3] Whig influence in some of the most vocal areas, notably the great manufacturing towns of the north, and, most of all, the metropolis, was negligible. The Whigs were more directly influential in the neighbourhood of their estates and their constituencies.

Clearly, the opposition's 'success' over the Property Tax in 1816 owed less to party mechanisms than might have been imagined. As with their success over the Orders in Council in 1812, the opposition had utilized the force of public opinion to reinforce its parliamentary proceedings. It was as if the parliamentary opposition had become an instrument of public impatience. The Whigs had encouraged the propertied middling orders to express their dislike of the tax, but they did not need the Whigs to tell them where their interests lay and how those interests might most readily be defended. At all events, in their anxiety to solicit public support, and thus to encourage vocal sections of the political nation to do away with the Property Tax, the opposition was marking a significant – and lasting – distinction between itself and a Tory government which was in economic and financial affairs more prudent and professional.

In defence of the opposition, it may be contended that the Whig party had historically argued the case for economy and that it had always deplored extravagance, inefficiency and corruption. In this sense, its opposition to the Property Tax was consistent with its opposition to the Army and Naval Estimates in 1816, for example, and with its attack on the extravagance of the government at the start of the 1817 session. The cry for Cheap Government was politically promising after the war. It did not matter – because it was not widely known – that the government had cut its expenditure to the bone, that the Civil List was being reduced and official salaries cut. Even though there was now arguably less validity in their allegations than ever before, the Whigs of the post-war years stood in a direct line of descent from the Rockingham Whigs in their crusade against corruption and for 'Economical Reform'. Such a campaign was no mere side-show. As the outcry against the Property Tax revealed, such issues could chime with the public's mood and even change government policy.

It is less helpful to catalogue the numerous occasions on which the opposition played the card of Cheap Government than to understand why they rarely played it effectively. Perhaps the most famous example of the opposition's inability is the catastrophic outcome of Tierney's State of the Nation motion on 8 May 1819 which, coming after months of vigorous and threatening activity, failed by a resounding 357 to 178. For one thing, the opposition's sense of timing was often awry – its

[3] A. Mitchell, *The Whigs in Opposition* (Oxford, 1967), p. 94.

tendency to introduce such motions late in the session is difficult to fathom. As we have already noticed, there was little confidence in the prospect of a Grey–Grenville government among many Parliamentarians. Most important of all, arguably, was the fact that many MPs hesitated to embark upon a witch-hunt against the government at a period when economic distress was provoking public agitation on a scale unknown since the 1790s.

The transition from a war-time to a peace-time economy severely strained social and economic relationships. The return of almost a third of a million men from active service to the labour market coincided with a sharp reduction in demand. The result was unemployment, aggravated by high prices for essential commodities. The subsequent economic hardship merged into political protest and agitation. The post-war distress lent considerable impetus to the popular radical movement led by Cobbett and Hunt. The pattern of agitation was, in the circumstances, remarkably orderly; strikes, marches and petitions passed off peacefully. It was the exceptions which terrorized the propertied classes; the Luddite outbreaks in the east midlands, the serious rural rioting in East Anglia and the infamous 'Spa Fields Riots' in London towards the end of 1816. The pathetic attempt upon the person of the Prince Regent in January 1817 stimulated the government to act. It immediately suspended Habeas Corpus and passed the Seditious Meetings Act after secret committees of both Houses had delivered their somewhat predictable verdicts upon some very dubious evidence.

Historians have long come to appreciate the circumstances in which the government acted; its lack of an efficient policing force to deal with riots, its dependence upon local agencies of law enforcement, its susceptibility to rumour and alarm and, not least, the persisting and terrifying example of the anarchy which had descended upon France in the 1790s. What reveals the government's political motives in 1817 was, however, not merely its repressive enactments, taken in isolation, but its endeavours to mobilize the propertied classes in their own defence, just as the loyalist Associations had done in the 1790s. The government acted not out of blind reaction but out of a quite natural desire to uphold the traditional orders and hierarchies of society. The autocracy of the government is less in evidence than its anxiety to mobilize the magistrates in its very politic desire to be seen to be acting firmly. The government's strategy was to take the political initiative and to weaken the connection between popular politics and social distress. The government did not believe that the mass of the people were disaffected. Liverpool and his ministers were concerned, however, that their simplicity left the people prey to politically minded agitators who could instigate panic and disorder which a constitutional government lacked the means of controlling. Thus the Seditious Meetings Act of 1817 attacked that classic tactic of the radicals, the mass meeting, with its popular excitement, its inflammatory vocabulary and its often militaristic overtones. There seems less need to argue whether Liverpool was right or wrong in the actions taken by his government in 1817 than to understand its anxieties and thus the specific objectives of its legislation. It was never its intention to inaugurate a reign of terror. The press remained untouched. The powers of local magistrates were scarcely utilized. All the 44 persons arrested by the government on suspicion of treason had been released by January 1818.

All this presented a fleeting target for the opposition to hit. The Whigs were no friends to popular agitators. Indeed, their denunciation of agitation once and for all convinced the radicals that the Whigs were unreliable allies. Be that as it may, some of them, Brougham particularly, wished to maintain their links with moderate and middle-class radicals like Burdett. They did not wish to lose this golden opportunity of attacking a government which seemed bent on destroying one of the hallowed planks of the Whig Platform, Habeas Corpus, and one of the sacred rights of Englishmen, the right of free assembly. The Whigs' resistance to the government's 'repressive' policies in 1817 was, notwithstanding, inhibited by their reluctance to appear to be defending revolutionaries, by their uncertain grasp of the public mood and by their own divisions. The main body of the party swallowed Grey's typically cautious, compromise line: to oppose the suspension of Habeas Corpus, to advocate the resolute exercise of the normal powers available to government and magistrates and to accept the principle of the Seditious Meeting Bill while opposing unnecessary and damaging restrictions on liberty. They kept their distance of the radicals during the session while vigorously opposing the suspension of Habeas Corpus, although members of their party had been included in the secret committees. Whig opposition, such as it was, therefore, consisted in lavish and wholly unconvincing denunciations of the despotic ambitions of the Liverpool ministry, together with old-fashioned constitutional maxims about liberty. In their hearts, however, the Whigs agreed with the government. In the last analysis, they stood closer to Liverpool than they stood to the radicals.

The revival of trade and the abundant harvest of 1817 took the sting out of the recession and quietened radical agitation more effectively than any amount of government legislation. The preconditions for agitation returned, however, in 1819. The radicals attempted to establish an extra-parliamentary convention but this was quickly vetoed by the government. Their subsequent tactic, that of holding mass meetings for the purpose of drawing up petitions to present to

Parliament, resulted in death, injury and martyrdom at the 'Peterloo Massacre' of 17 August 1819. After a powerful extra-parliamentary campaign, led and organized by the Whig opposition, protesting against the Massacre, the government felt that it had no alternative but to adopt a firm stance against present and future agitations. The government decided to clarify the law on illegal assemblies while discouraging future mass meetings. The Six Acts regulated public meetings and laid down the procedure for prosecutions in cases arising out of them. More contentiously, the acts encouraged and permitted magistrates to search for arms and to seize seditious publications. Significantly, they extended duties payable on newspapers and periodicals.

It is difficult to recreate the atmosphere of panic which gripped the ruling establishment at the time. There can be no doubt that the radicals had succeeded in awakening the attention of a lower-class audience. What disturbed ministers were not the wild stories about imminent insurrection but the apparently ineluctable spread of agitation and the willingness of the parliamentary opposition to sponsor and to champion its advance. The government's response, while speedy, was carefully considered: 'The Whigs were as much the intended victims of the Six Acts as the Radicals.'[4]

The Acts passed through Parliament by the end of the year with little amendment, a gratifying reassurance to the government that the instincts of most MPs were sound. Parliament clearly accepted the sound Tory case which the ministers made in debate that their answer to Peterloo was in the best interests of the country, its stability, its property and its institutions. The Acts, they argued, were consistent with the constitutional conventions of the nation, not inimical to them. Their aim was to break the link that was believed to exist between unavoidable and regrettable distress and political agitation. This was the justification both for the Act which affected the press and another which forbade unauthorized military assemblies. In any case, the Act prohibiting mass meetings for political purposes, like that exhorting magistrates to search for arms, was a temporary measure only. In the circumstances, such precautions were eminently reasonable and moderate.

The Whig opposition saw things very differently. Their reaction to government repression was somewhat more principled than it had been in 1817 and they leapt to the defence of popular liberties with commendable conviction. It is not at once easy to understand why their attitude should have changed so markedly within two years. No doubt Peterloo was a more sensational piece of political symbolism than the

[4] J.E. Cookson, *Lord Liverpool's Administration* (1975), p. 186.

Spa Fields Riots. Perhaps, too, they had learned something from the General Election of 1818. This first peace-time election since 1790 had been a modest but encouraging success for the Whigs. They had picked up about 30 seats and were clearly more closely in tune with the public mood than the government. Their success may have done something to assuage their doubts about public opinion. It certainly stiffened the fibre of Grey and Tierney and encouraged them to believe that they could lead and control the popular voice. They took a sterner line with the radicals, seized the initiative from them, and assumed the task of finding a middle way between radicals and government.

The Whigs, in spite of some hesitation and characteristic dithering, made a good job of making political and party capital out of Peterloo. They placed themselves at the head of the protest movement and appealed to the country. Yet again, they repeated the pattern of protest utilized in 1812 and 1816, using meetings, speeches and petitions with which to attack the government and reinforce their own standing with the public. Although only nine county meetings could be held before Parliament met, numerous town meetings took place. In short, the Whigs made an effective appeal to a public opinion already sympathetic to the victims of Peterloo. On the eve of the new session of Parliament the party was more united, more vigorous and more popular than at any time since the early 1790s.

Yet the stronger it became, the more ineffective it was. For in laying down such a clear and direct challenge to the prestige and reputation of the government, the Whigs were forcing it to legislate, and to carry its supporters in Parliament along with that legislation. Government and opposition were thus locked into a battle from which they could not escape. The government retorted to the opposition's demand for an enquiry into Peterloo by forcing the Six Acts through Parliament. This it did with considerable success. Nevertheless, the Whigs did conspicuously better in their parliamentary opposition than they had done in 1817, dividing on the important motions at around 150.

By early 1820 the government had its legislation but by then the affairs of Queen Caroline had overtaken the nationwide preoccupation with Peterloo. The death of George III in January 1820 threatened to precipitate a new crisis for Liverpool. The new King would not tolerate the prospect that his wife, Queen Caroline, who had in recent years lived a scandalous existence abroad, might return to Britain to claim her rights as Consort. Her legal advisor was none other than Henry Brougham, whose ambition ensured that the resulting scandal would be smeared with partisan political overtones. The new King forced the ministers to agree to help him to divorce his wife. Inconveniently, however, she turned up in London on 6 June 1820 and brought the affair at once to a crisis. Last minute attempts to reach some compromise between King and Queen came to nothing. Thereupon, the ministers introduced a Bill to dissolve the marriage. The public parliamentary enquiry which accompanied these proceedings continued from August to November. After a series of unedifying revelations, in which the Queen appeared to the public as a (not altogether deserving) persecuted martyr, the ministers were able to push their Bill through the Lords with a narrow majority. It would have little chance in the Commons. Consequently they bowed to the inevitable and dropped the Bill. It was Liverpool's worst defeat since the Property Tax of 1816.

It was indeed a nightmare for Liverpool. Rather unfairly, the government, rather than the monarch, was the object of widespread popular vilification in 1820. It never really recovered its composure and its demoralization led directly to the reconstruction of the ministry in the early 1820s. Nevertheless, it is important to remember that throughout the crisis, and even in an area of royal and not merely ministerial concern, the government and not the monarch took most of the important decisions. The King might, in his tantrums, threaten to abdicate or to sack his ministers but they were ready and able to stand up to him and ready to take decisions which were extremely distasteful to him.

As for the opposition, they took up the Queen's case, ultimately voting against the Bill of divorce, with some reluctance. Many of the more senior men of the party found the affair sordid and distasteful and wished at first to preserve an Olympian detachment. This feeling could not endure. After all, Brougham had already given them an interest in the proceedings. The affairs of the royal family, especially when as spectacularly unsavoury as they now were, could hardly be ignored. If this were not enough, the public sympathy for the Queen made it inevitable that they should support her cause. There was good party advantage in it. As Brougham put it: she was 'a Constitutional means of making head against a revenue of 105 millions, an army of half a million, and 800 millions of debt.' In any case, their longstanding dislike of the Regent helped to remove any remaining scruples. So Caroline became a sort of reversionary interest which the Whigs could use against the monarchy and against the government, as they had used the same George who was now King almost 40 years earlier.

Not surprisingly, the opposition's advocacy of the Queen's case confirmed the new King's distaste for them and renewed their proscription from office. For all their factiousness – it is not at all easy to decide how seriously the opposition really believed the constitution to be threatened by what the ministers were proposing – the opposition was mounting a challenge to George IV. It was telling him that his private affairs were not merely matters of high public concern but that they would be both ready and anxious to thwart him over those affairs. Indeed, their support of the Queen seriously embarrassed the ministers in Parliament and made it even more daunting for them to proceed with the Bill.

As on several occasions in recent years, the Whigs emerged as the champions of public opinion. They did not create the massive sympathy for the Queen which swept the country in 1820 but it was second nature for them, by now, to wish to exploit it and to control it. They raised almost a dozen petitions from county meetings and somewhat hurriedly endeavoured to direct sentiment in their localities. It was, however, both too widespread and too tumultuous for them to control it. The Caroline agitation threw up a remarkable torrent of propaganda which was clearly designed to appeal to the lower orders. Indeed, men of humble station joined the massive demonstrations which were widespread, especially in the metropolis. This made the affair doubly worrying for ministers. It was not only a first rate political scandal. It threatened the security of the capital and the preservation of law and order as well as the government.

Nevertheless, the Whigs were, in the last analysis, unable to remove the government. Their lack of success, and the ministry's remarkable ability to reconstruct and to renew itself in the succeeding months should not conceal the importance of these years in the development of party politics. In spite of their regular confrontations, government and opposition shared much common ground. Furthermore, on many of the issues agitated in these years the superficial polarities of politics conceal serious divisions *within* both government and opposition. These may have obscured the definition of party programmes. Nevertheless, the experiences of these years served to extend participation in politics from the traditional parliamentary classes down into the middling orders and beyond. This incorporation of public opinion into party politics no doubt proceeded from a variety of motives, many of them unquestionably patrician and thus proceeding from the assumption that the existing structure of power should remain undisturbed. Yet it was to be a permanent consolidation of popular elements and popular strategies within the framework of party politics. A period of economic prosperity now intervened, to an extent unknown since before 1789. The consequent diminution of social unrest should not conceal the fact that these political advances were to be permanent. Already politicians were cutting the path that was to lead to 1832 and, unknowingly, to anticipate the prospects presented by parliamentary reform.

Party and Parliament: 1820–27

Between the Caroline affair and the end of Liverpool's ministry political conflict was normally confined to the cockpit of Parliament. After the years of excitement, distress and the consequent extra-parliamentary eruptions into the traditional political world, passions subsided and politics settled into the peaceful period of so-called 'Liberal–Tory' reforms.

After the tensions of the Caroline affair, however, the ministry needed to be reconstructed. Indeed, there was initially some doubt as to whether it could continue. The King hoped not. He was disenchanted with ministers who had been unwilling to follow his instructions. His soundings with the opposition showed, however, that they were unable and unwilling to come to his rescue. He allowed Liverpool to continue but would not have Canning back in the cabinet.[5] Liverpool had to accept the bitter pill. Indeed, he had little choice, especially as the bulk of the cabinet probably would have sided with the King. For all that, changes had to come. In the next few months, Peel replaced Sidmouth at the Home Office, Robinson became Chancellor of the Exchequer and Huskisson became President of the Board of Trade. In 1821 the Grenvilles returned to office, amidst the expected flurry of offices and honours. After Castlereagh's suicide in August 1822 there was no alternative to Canning at the Foreign Office and, like his predecessor, he became Leader of the House of Commons, the inheritance for which he had yearned since 1812. By the end of 1822 the pieces were in place.

The subsequent years have conventionally been described as a period of 'Liberal–Toryism'. Little violence is done to the reality of government policy so long as we recognize that the ministry's objectives in economic policy underwent little significant change, that many of the policies concerned were already under contemplation or had even been introduced or anticipated before 1820 and that the men who implemented 'Liberal–Toryism' were already in government before 1820. What was new, of course, was the climate of prosperity and optimism which enabled the government to legislate, free of the immediate concerns of social unrest. Ministers were thus able to devote the bulk of their time and energies to problems of financial reconstruction and commercial growth.

What may also be discerned after 1820 is a firmer grasp of the nettle of leadership. It took some time for ministers to reassert their control over the Commons. The General Election of 1820 had favoured the opposition rather than the government and the new Parliament was at

---

[5] Canning had resigned from the ministry in 1820 because he believed that ministers were unfairly and unnecessarily persecuting the Queen.

first fractious and awkward to handle. The government had to face a series of attacks from a number of groups, from currency reformers, protectionists, from retrenchment radicals as well as from the Whig opposition. The worst moment for Liverpool came when in the session of 1821 a group of dissatisfied agriculturalists ganged up with the opposition to repeal the tax on farm horses. The Prime Minister was having no more nonsense. The government put its foot down. If the revenue of the country were to be the victim of further capricious opposition then it would resign. Thereafter, Parliament became noticeably easier to manage; but even in these great years of Liverpool, it remained an unreliable assembly. Lingering dissatisfaction with the government provoked an alliance of Tory squires, radicals and Whigs in the following session which attempted to repeal the tax on salt. The government saved the Salt Tax by only four votes. On 7 March 1821 it even suffered the humiliation of losing on a proposal to establish a Committee of Enquiry into the State of Agriculture. In the end, the Committee became something of a platform for free traders but the government had been dealt a salutary shock.

Such reverses did not prevent the ministry from proceeding with its hosts of Bills and resolutions, often on specific and sometimes extremely technical topics. The policy of 'Liberal–Toryism', in short, amounted to a policy of cutting taxes, reducing interest rates, removing restrictions on trade, reducing or removing tariffs, furthering free trade between Britain and the colonies and, in general, promoting national economic expansion over and against sectional interests. The great financial crisis of 1825 found the government characteristically willing to regulate and reform the banking system, the abuses of which had been responsible for the run on the banks, while being unwilling to indulge in measures of protection and paternalism. The rash of discussion provoked by the crisis led to further anguished debate upon the legitimacy of the government's economic policy. Sectional interests apart, few compelling arguments were offered against the government's position: that structural changes in the British economy were desirable to harness the new forces of manufacture and commerce, that protection led to backwardness and lack of innovation and that British international power depended for its successful enlargement upon the strength of the nation's economic base.

This last objective was increasingly the ultimate objective of British foreign policy under Canning. Castlereagh's great State Paper of 5 May 1820 had already laid it down that 'this country cannot and will not act upon abstract and speculative Principles of Precaution.' Canning perceived that it was in Britain's economic interests not to attempt to police Europe and the world, as some continental leaders envisaged, but to trade as widely as possible. In this context, it was peculiarly in Britain's interests to permit and to promote political change which benefited the national interest. The collapse of the Spanish empire in the New World provoked one of the outstanding themes of British foreign policy in the 1820s; whether the government ought to recognize the emergent republics. Canning bided his time, but President Monroe's willingness to fish in troubled waters brought him to recognize their independence at the end of 1824. It was not long before trade treaties with these new commercial partners were being negotiated.

In the years of the ministry of the Younger Pitt prior to the outbreak of war with France in 1793, the peaceful pursuit of economic expansion at home and abroad had met with a favourable response from the opposition. Now, a similar consensus on economic and foreign affairs diluted the bitterness of party politics in the 1820s. 'From 89 divisions in which government and opposition had clashed in 1822 the number dwindled to 59 in 1823, 56 in 1824, 29 in 1825 and 20 in 1826.'[6] On some issues, the government depended upon opposition votes for its security. Changes to the Corn Law in 1827 were stoutly resisted by the country gentlemen but carried with the help of opposition votes. In the same session the opposition refused to harass the government factiously over its financial policy. As had happened on previous occasions, periods of prosperity and stability were taking the sting out of party politics, the voice of the public was muted and the only great constitutional issue of the time, Catholic Emancipation, was something more than a party issue.

Nevertheless, the impetus towards the growing cohesion of government and opposition parties was not entirely lost. Although the opposition may have been losing something of its own cohesion as a party in the 1820s – this is still debated among historians – perceptible advances were made towards greater cohesion in the government majority. It was to some extent inevitable that a long ministry would generate its own continuity and cohesion, in sharp contradistinction to the short-lived ministries of the period 1801–12. Nevertheless, it was in part the essential weakness rather than the strength of the position of ministers which led to these developments. There was less patronage available to ensure a government majority and, what was worse, Liverpool was averse to using what there was – especially church patronage – for overtly political purposes. By this time, moreover, only about 80 MPs held office of the government. Another score or two for personal or political reasons might have been counted unconditional government supporters. The rest of government's majority

[6] A. Mitchell, *op. cit.*, p. 183.

needed to be managed with the greatest care and sensitivity. For ministers did not claim the right to force Members against their wishes. In any case, they lacked appropriate sanctions with which to punish them. Most MPs inclined to support the government were not dependent upon it for their seat in Parliament. And in the absence of nationally organized, bureaucratic party machines, Members enjoyed considerable freedom. Furthermore, although something over 250 MPs professed to support government, and, in practice, did so on all critical occasions, as we have seen, they were not bound to a party programme or to a series of measures. In the last analysis, however, they were committed to maintaining Liverpool in office and to keeping the Whigs out. It is less significant that they were prepared to oppose the government on a particular measure than that they were consistently prepared to sustain it on issues of confidence.

Nevertheless, there are signs that by the early 1820s – and to some extent the ministerial changes of those years may have played some part here – ministers were planning and co-ordinating their legislation much more efficiently than hitherto. A more professional attitude was replacing the more languid ministerial habits of the eighteenth century. Correspondingly, the organization of the government majority was becoming rather more sophisticated. Castlereagh (1812–22) and Canning (1822–7) were active and charismatic Leaders of the House of Commons. Their duties as Foreign Secretary, however, required that they should delegate to others the routine business of parliamentary management. Charles Arbuthnot was Joint Secretary to the Treasury. His work as patronage secretary, involving the distribution and promise of offices and favours, helped to ensure that ministers were not more sorely tried than they were. Furthermore, the business of bringing members to town and to the House was becoming a fairly sophisticated activity by the 1820s. Government Whips were by now salaried officials. The Chief Whip, William Holmes, was assisted by a group of Treasury officials. Between them, Arbuthnot and the Whips circulated letters to government supporters, advising them of the meeting of Parliament and the order of business, requesting their attendance and advising them how to vote. Such exertions were still less than routine. They represented the government's reaction to trouble or to anticipated trouble. They were not yet the normal, conventional methods of disciplining a party majority, although they represented interesting anticipations of later methods.

Government was able to manage without elaborate and formal machinery because it did not need it. The customary ingredients of ministerial power were sufficient for most purposes and contemporary opinion would not have tolerated ministerial attempts to erode local privileges and freedoms. For example, the government did not fight elections in any thoroughly co-ordinated manner. There is little evidence of centralized direction in the affairs of local election committees. Government Whips, it is true, had a general and somewhat ambiguous responsibility for general elections but they did not have many resources. They might be able to send a little money to a few friendly candidates. They might be able to make use of Treasury, Army and Admiralty influence in the few score boroughs where it still endured as a significant electoral factor, but, in the last analysis, ministers were dependent upon their local supporters, especially local families of weight and reputation, for the return of friendly candidates.

Yet again, the weaknesses of politicians led to innovation. The harsh truth was that the traditional components of ministerial influence upon elections were dwindling away. Curwen's Act of 1809 forbade the purchase of parliamentary seats and the cautious Liverpool would not attempt to defy it. Furthermore, the money traditionally expended upon elections from the Privy Purse and the Secret Service Fund had almost disappeared. At the election of 1826 some rationalization of election organization appeared in the form of a committee of management which conducted the government's campaign and attempted to co-ordinate its activities. It performed, in short, the sort of activities for the government which Adam had performed for the opposition in the 1780s. It would, of course, be far-fetched to announce this unassuming body as the first evidence of an autonomous Tory party separate from ministerial influence. Its appearance does, however, suggest how the deficiencies of the latter gradually summoned the former into existence.

The developing cohesion of the government party in the 1820s is not to be measured solely by organizational criteria but also by its political relationships. As we have seen, there was no love lost between ministers and monarch after the Caroline affair. In December 1820, in fact, George IV went so far as to ask Grenville to form a government. Liverpool had some reason to feel threatened and, thereafter, uneasy. Consequently, he tried to establish the principle that private favour alone was inadequate recommendation for public office. He went even further and at times came close to the doctrine that the King's appointment to cabinet offices should take account of the advice of the cabinet. Liverpool did not succeed in making his point. After all, the King kept Canning out of the cabinet for years and had much to do with keeping Sidmouth in until 1824. In the long run, however, after all the royal tantrums had subsided and the political quarrels had been composed, Lord Liverpool controlled the personnel of his administration and, to a large extent, its policies.

In the eighteenth century the King had been the first of party leaders and royal, not party, government prevailed. Now, a King's party no longer existed, the King was no longer the first of party leaders and his powers were being gradually curtailed. A Tory party organized on modern, bureaucratic lines had not yet appeared in the early 1820s but the conditions of its growth were steadily emerging. By the 1820s, then, Liverpool was acting on assumptions rather similar to those of the Whigs. His government relied less on royal favour than upon its own strengths and merits, his own indispensability and the probability that, had he resigned, he would surely not have resigned alone. George IV would have had no alternative but to bring in the Whigs. In theory, it was a King's government not a party one. The reality was vastly different.[7]

The fundamental inspiration of Liverpool's government, however, was less a party ideology than a broad and unifying ideal. It may be argued – and with some force – that the objectives of the Liverpool ministry were essentially Tory. In the post-war years the tidal wave of revulsion against radical agitation and in favour of repressive legislation, together with the Anglican reaction against Catholic and Dissenting aspirations can be described in no other way. Yet Toryism was not a party creed and the Liverpool ministry cannot be regarded as its sole vehicle. Powerful Tory traditions existed, for example, which utterly repudiated the *laissez-faire* direction of the ministry in the 1820s and even before. In the 1820s the Liverpool ministry was pursuing a combination of Tory objectives and traditional ministerial goals in an all-inclusive rather than exclusively party manner.

Nevertheless, the ministry could not have survived without its growing organizational apparatus, its acceptance of conventions of party conflict at Westminster and its readiness to employ techniques of party organization and propaganda in the extra-parliamentary arena. By the 1820s all but the most hidebound traditionalist had come to accept the need and necessity for parties as a support to government, as the basis of opposition and as the ultimate guarantee of the liberties of the country and the balance of the constitution. Upon this foundation could be erected the later conventions of party alternation in government.

The opposition party in Parliament was longer established than that on the other side of the House but, lacking the focus of power and office, was even less firmly led. It is not too much to say that the Whig party existed without effective leadership until 1830. Lord Grey had

[7] The decline of the monarchy did not automatically entail the triumph of party or even of parliamentary government. The immediate beneficiary was the Cabinet. In the eighteenth century cabinet ministers had been links between the King and Parliament, appointed by him but removable either by him or by Parliament. By the 1820s the Cabinet had taken the political initiative away from the King and was attempting, sometimes vainly it is true, to control Parliament.

neither the energy nor the courage to lend direction or initiative to the opposition. He was essentially a leisurely conciliator. As his party's prospects worsened after 1820 he grew ever more aloof and distant until in 1824 he retreated from politics, leaving Lansdowne to be treated as his successor – a high-handed and patrician gesture in which the Whig party nevertheless acquiesced. To be fair to Grey, he was cursed with ill-health, as was his wife. Indeed, the ostensible reason for his 'retirement' was his wish to nurse her back to health. Lansdowne, hitherto a pleasant and lively peer, crumbled under the responsibility of leadership; indeed, he spent most of his time stifling initiatives and advising caution. After the death of Ponsonby in 1817 George Tierney became leader of the opposition in the Lower House and the pulse of opposition began to quicken. It perhaps says something for the tenor of Whig politics in the lower House, however, that it required a petition circulated by the opposition Whips among the party in the Commons to persuade Tierney to accept. Tierney set about his task with energy and vigour. His failure to topple the government in 1818–19, weakened his authority and his health. Thereafter Tierney was leader in name only. The party drifted leaderless until, in 1830, after yet another petition, the leadership in the Commons passed to Lord Althorp, a man acceptable to most elements in the party. At that point the question of the Whig leadership merged into somewhat wider questions concerning the future of the Whig party and of the electoral system.

Deficiencies in leadership were not compensated by developments in organization. The party did not believe in and did not yearn for centralized organization any more than it demanded vigorous leadership. Their own natural indolence, the hopelessness of their political prospects and the lukewarmness of their political associates restrained the Whigs from excesses of activity. The organizational framework pioneered by Adam was no longer functioning as efficiently as it had in the 1780s, partly because the existence of the opposition was appreciably more secure than it had been at that time, but it did continue to operate.

To summon men to Parliament opposition Whips sent letters to members of the Whig party. (The Grenvilles had their own Whip and organization.) James MacDonald acted as Chief Whip for the opposition until he left Parliament in 1816. He was replaced in a more formal capacity by Lord Duncannon, who retained the post until 1830. He comes closer than anyone in this period to imitating Adam's achievement. He was involved not only in whipping but in electoral management, sessional planning and discussions over personnel. Confusingly, however, the Whips were only as good as the leaders in both Houses. All the Whips could do was to canvass members once they were in town. It was up to the Leaders to bring them to town in the first place.

One particularly important further function for the Whips was to organize party meetings. These were held much more frequently than meetings of government supporters and may help to explain, whatever their other failings, the familiarity often evinced by the leading men of the opposition with the opinions of their followers.[8]

The efficient collection and expenditure of money had been characteristics of Adam's administration of the party in the 1780s. Here again, his legacy had not been preserved. Apart from a sudden flurry of activity in 1806–7, the party funds do not seem to have operated with much regularity. Money for electioneering was lacking and consequently co-ordinated election campaigns could not be fought. Election subscriptions might be launched for particularly prestigious contests – Brougham's successive attempts at Westmorland after 1818, Romilly's endeavours at Bristol, Whitbread's at Middlesex in 1820 and the Westminster elections of 1818 and 1820 – but there was little overall co-ordination.

Similarly, the party was less active in organizing press publicity than it had been in the 1780s. By now, however, there was less need for it since newspaper support was arising spontaneously and informally. *The Morning Chronicle*, under its editor, James Perry, was closely enmeshed in party activities. Until his death in 1821, the *Chronicle* was the great advocate of Foxite Whiggism and Perry one of its most influential apologists. In addition, about one half of the London papers in the early nineteenth century were sympathetic to the opposition.[9]

Outside Parliament, the organizational fortunes of the opposition were located in various quarters. Brooks Club, with its exclusively Whig membership, remained the social focus of the Whig political elite in the metropolis. A more select group inhabited the classical setting of Holland House to manufacture and to perpetuate the myth of Fox. More widely, however, the Whig Club had become the effective organ of Whig party organization throughout the country. The Whig Club had steadily developed in importance down to the end of the 1790s, when it could boast around 1,000 members, two-thirds of them outside the metropolis. After 1800, the central body began to spawn a score or so of provincial equivalents. These co-existed with the metropolitan and provincial Fox Clubs, which prospered for some two decades after Fox's death and then began to decline. (Perhaps surprisingly, Pitt Clubs were somewhat more widespread and more permanent.) This was the extent of the opposition's extra-Parliamentary organization. It

---

[8] Dr Mitchell has counted no fewer than 28 such meetings between 1815 and 1828 (*The Whigs in Opposition*, p. 42).
[9] I.R. Christie, *Myth and Reality in Late Eighteenth Century British Politics* (Macmillan, 1970), p. 328.

was an identifiable if somewhat informal, anticipation of the organizational advances of the 1830s.

As for issues, the years were beginning to lumber the Whig opposition with a growing list of commitments, many of them shouldered willingly enough at the outset, less consistently thereafter. Nevertheless, there can be little doubting their sincerity in opposing the government's repressive policies in the post-war years. Such an attitude was consistent with the old Rockinghamite distrust of the executive and strongly reminiscent of Fox's stand for civil liberties in the mid 1790s. Their commitment to repeal the Combination Laws stood in the same tradition. Almost as historic were their commitments to Protestant Dissenters to repeal the Test and Corporation Acts and to the Catholics to pursue Catholic Emancipation. The Whigs may with some justice be criticized for failing to prosecute these objectives as vigorously as they might have done. What is less contentious is the overall cohesion of the various elements of their programme. The cardinal element in early nineteenth century Whiggism was its insistence upon *political* liberty. All other liberties were predicated upon the assumption of political liberty. Thus, Whig foreign policy, Whig resistance to the Six Acts, Whig defence of Habeas Corpus and of the press form a reasoned corpus of political ideology. This insistence upon *political* liberty, and the good offices of the Whig aristocracy in establishing and defending it, helps to explain the neglect among the opposition of many of the newer economic and social problems of the age. The confusion and indifference over economic and financial issues to be found among the opposition to Liverpool may also be attributed less to Whig wilfulness than to the limitations of Whig ideology.

An essential component of Whig ideology since the early 1790s had been parliamentary reform. Most writers have, with considerable justification, castigated the Whigs for their lukewarm attachment to reform. After 1797 their commitment lapsed in the face of massive, popular hostility. In fact, they fell back upon the convenient decision to wait for the public mood to change before they would advocate reform systematically. The coalition with Grenville did much to dilute the party's enthusiasm yet further. Indeed, some of its leaders, Holland and Fitzwilliam for example, were delighted that they could now disregard indefinitely the inconvenient and unpopular measure to which the party had become wedded in the 1790s under the immediate inspiration of reform movements and radical agitation. Most fatal of all for the prospects for reform, Grey was unsympathetic, languid and pessimistic as to its prospects.

As the pressure from radicals for parliamentary discussion began to grow in the early years of the nineteenth century Grey's resistance provoked some of the younger men in the party to go their own way. On 21

May 1810 Thomas Brand moved for a committee to consider the issue of reform. The respectable minority of 115 against 234 showed that parliamentary reform was perceptibly less unpopular among MPs than it had been for many years. Circumstances, however, prevented young bloods like Samuel Whitbread, William Smith and Thomas Brand from converting the party to reform. Its solicitousness for the sensitivities of the Prince Regent in the vital years 1811–12 needs no underlining. It was not until the end of the war and, just as important, the end of radical agitation after it, that some change in the outlook of the Whig party grandees might be expected. Until then, constant attacks upon the system of influence and advocacy of retrenchment and economical reform would have to suffice.

Even in this period, however, the Whig party never entirely abandoned its belief in its historic function to moderate between the forces of ministerial despotism and radical anarchy by providing statesmanlike leadership for propertied men of the middling orders. The popular agitation not only underlined this historic function. It provided impressive evidence of the conversion of the middling orders to reform. During the session of 1817 an astonishing 700 petitions from 350 towns were forthcoming on the subject of reform alone. The convergence of sentiment between the opposition and public opinion between 1815 and 1820 did much to diminish its earlier, somewhat hysterical, fears of the people. In pushing them back towards its earlier commitment to reform, however, we should not underestimate the importance of the activities of a knot of young aristocrats who were to play a critical role in 1832. These included Russell, Althorp, and Milton, above all, but also Tavistock and Ebrington.

Grey could see what was happening. Now that conditions in the country were changing and a more liberal spirit becoming apparent, some sections of the party were turning to parliamentary reform. He was coming to see that the party could not afford indefinitely to alienate the rising force of opinion among the respectable and propertied middling orders. By the end of 1820 Grey himself had in mind a scheme to abolish the most corrupt 100 boroughs and to redistribute the seats to the populous towns and counties. If there is a particular occasion when the party positively committed itself to parliamentary reform as an immediate priority, however, it was on Russell's reform resolution in April 1822. The division, 269 to 164, clearly indicated that parliamentary reform was no longer the concern of a small minority of members, which it had been for nearly 40 years. Many took the occasion to declare for reform. Grey saw that the Whigs must henceforward promise and deliver a substantial scheme of parliamentary reform. At just this moment, the return of prosperity nipped these developments in the bud. Even so, Russell actually obtained five votes more for a further reform motion a year later.

Lack of support in the country inhibited him from making further efforts during the next few years. Even in the unfavourable year of 1826, however, his motion for reform attracted a respectable 123 against 247. If prosperity should break or if the stability of the ministry should be upset, then the Whigs were ready. And it is, of course, not difficult to see why they were ready. By the early 1820s, it was becoming frighteningly clear to the Whigs that their best endeavours had not seriously shaken the government, that office was as far away as ever, that antagonism and conflict accompanied their uneasy relations with the radicals and, cruellest of all, that opinion in the country was swinging back towards Liverpool. It was less their popularity than their lack of it which convinced the Whigs that the reform of the representation might be in their own interest.

Under the existing system, they seemed doomed to a period of indefinite opposition and scarcely looked like a credible alternative government. They still suffered royal proscription. The hatred which George IV bore them for their support of Caroline needs little fresh emphasis. What is much less frequently acknowledged is the reluctance of the Whigs to associate themselves with other members of the royal family and assume a reversionary interest in successive heirs to the throne. The Duke of York, heir to the throne between 1817 and 1827, detested the Whigs and their Catholic policies and would have nothing to do with them. During these years the Whigs at last began to realize that their political salvation was not to be sought through a reversionary interest and that they had probably harmed themselves through such relationships in the past. If the Whigs were to return to power it must be as a result of a vote in the House of Commons and not of a royal manoeuvre.

During normal times, however, the Whigs found it difficult to maintain the role of a credible alternative government. Continual harassment of the ministry and obstruction of its business, while possibly effective, was unpopular and could appear factious. The opposition did best when it concentrated on the great political, constitutional and religious issues, such as the defence of liberties and Catholic Emancipation. This latter held some promise. Throughout Liverpool's ministry Catholic Emancipation was an open question in the cabinet and it was supported by, among others, Canning and Grenville: Even more important, it commanded considerable support from all quarters in the House of Commons. The trouble was that on such issues the opposition frequently did not do as well as it might have done. Its own divisions, its timid leadership and lethargic strategy and the basic reluctance of the majority of MPs to see a Whig government in office condemned them to indefinite opposition.

The years of Liverpool's ministry, however, finally broke Whig ties with the Grenvilles and ended the inhibitions upon their development as a party which the coalition had imposed. On the issues of popular agitation and law and order after 1815 the Grenvilles had been anxious to support, not to attack, the government. Coincidentally, the death of Ponsonby in 1817 removed one of the most regular means of communication and concert between the Whigs and the Grenvilles. By this time, Lord Grenville himself was withdrawing from politics. His personal relationship with Grey had done much to keep the Coalition together. Now, the Duke of Buckingham assumed the leadership of the Grenville clan. He had three characteristics. He hated the Whigs, he wished for office for himself and his relations and he was completely reactionary in his politics. In 1818 the Grenvilles separated themselves from the opposition by becoming a Third Party. In 1822 they joined Liverpool's administration. Charles Fox's coalition with the Grenvilles had at last been undone. In spite of their manifest deficiencies, the Whigs of the 1820s were returning to the platform of the 1790s, the inhibitions of the Napoleonic Wars and the Grenville coalition now removed. The seeds of the 1790s, indeed, were to be theirs to harvest.

The Confusion of Parties: 1827–30

The paralytic stroke which removed Lord Liverpool from politics in February 1827 inaugurated five years of political turbulence. These were only ended with the Reform Act of 1832. During this period both parties underwent major divisions and realignments. By the end of it, both had repaired their damaged cohesion and were preparing to adjust themselves to the new electoral world in which they now had to live. The ability of the parties to ride out the political upheavals of these years says much for their strength as parties and for the extent to which politics was hardening in a two-party mould before 1832.

The departure of a long-serving Prime Minister usually precipitated political confusion. This had been so at the fall of North in 1782 and at that of Pitt in 1801. But these precedents shrank into insignificance compared to what happened in 1827. Within weeks, both major parties were shattered. Lord Liverpool was replaced by George Canning. Canning died in August 1827 to be replaced, in turn, by Goderich. His inability to command respect led the Duke of Wellington to assume the Premiership in January 1828. These 'succession ministries' 'represented the fragmentation of the old governmental connection rather than any new alignment.'[10] Personal and political weaknesses drained

[10] N. Gash, *Aristocracy and People* (1979), p. 129.

them of authority. They were unable to withstand the shock-waves generated by the great issues of the late 1820s – Repeal of the Test and Corporation Acts, Catholic Emancipation and Parliamentary Reform. By late 1830 the way was clear for Grey's Whig party to take office on a platform of Parliamentary Reform.

George IV had replaced Liverpool with Canning with good reason. Canning commanded the Commons, most Tory MPs wanted him and the King knew that Canning would take nothing less than the Premiership. Canning, moreover, was popular out of doors. His appointment would combine royal convenience and parliamentary assent with public approval.

In fact, it caused Wellington, Peel, Eldon and four others to resign from the cabinet and it prompted no fewer than 35 resignations among the minor office-holders. The most common reason given for their resignation was that Canning was an advocate of Catholic Emancipation. But Canning had no intention of promoting Catholic Emancipation as a government measure and he was content for the issue to remain an 'open' question in the cabinet. To understand why so many leading politicians refused to support the minister of the King's choice – no small matter in the early nineteenth century – we must look elsewhere.

In fact, we need to examine the growing suspicions and anxieties of large numbers of Tories about the direction in which their party was being led. Although it may be fashionable to treat right-wing Ultra Tories with scant respect because they lost the political battles of this period – over the Repeal of the Test and Corporation Acts, over Catholic Emancipation and over Parliamentary Reform – we should underestimate neither their numbers, nor their strength, nor their passionate sincerity. In repudiating the minister of the King's choice they were holding out the traditional principles of their party over and against the respect traditionally due to the monarchy. In other words, their fears for the Protestant Constitution overcame the respect which they normally allowed to the monarchy.

The revolt against Canning, therefore, was far more than an expression of dislike of an individual, however controversial and high-handed he might be. It was the culmination of a quietly gathering current of opinion within the Tory party and one which needs to be taken into account if the party's development during the next few years is to be understood. Throughout the 1820s Tory 'Protestants' (those against Repeal and Emancipation) and agriculturalists had been unable to persuade the House of Commons to reflate the currency, to arrest the trend to free trade, to reinforce agricultural protection and to repeal the Malt Tax. Now, the prospect of an attack on the Anglican Constitution was too much. The deep tensions within the Tory party had been concealed during the later years of his ministry by Liverpool's own mastery of the conciliatory arts. But even before his removal from politics, his ministry was experiencing defections in the division lobby with dangerous regularity and coming to depend upon Whig votes for the successful passage of its legislation. Between 1824 and 1827 there was constant friction in the party over Corn and Catholics. With Liverpool's removal in 1827 the old Tory party lost these right-wing Ultras.

The political vacuum thus created on the ministerial side of the House was filled by a small group from within the Whig party. Arguing that liberal principles should be supported wherever they were to be found and, no doubt, comforted in their action by their belief that little use would be served by an extended period of opposition, four Whigs (Lansdowne, Devonshire, Tierney and Lamb), took places in Canning's cabinet. Others offered support from outside. This alliance between the liberal Tories and the Whigs (or, at least, some of them) promised to realign British politics during the ministries of Canning and Goderich on the basis of liberals *v.* Ultras and reactionaries.

There can be no denying the opportunist nature of these initiatives. Well might Grey publicly accuse his colleagues of deserting their party principles, of failing to seek assurances on Repeal – which was to be resisted by the ministry – and on Emancipation – which was to remain an open question. Furthermore, they had simply grabbed whatever Canning had offered them. Rockingham and Fox would have wept in their graves. The anarchy of every man for himself was just what party government was intended to prevent, not promote.

Grey need not have worried. The great venture collapsed. Lansdowne and his colleagues were unhappy in office under Canning and Goderich. They found that it was they, rather than the Canningites and the King, who were having to make the concessions and compromises. When Wellington's ministry superseded Goderich's, the Whigs returned to the opposition benches, which they had for so long occupied, in evident embarrassment. Wellington was able to patch together the old Liverpool coalition and to work with both Canningites and Ultras. The Tories had been reunited; the Whigs had been dished. The only honourable route to office was that which Grey continued to advocate; the defeat of a ministry in the House of Commons by united party action.

Indeed, Grey had by no means been alone in holding himself aloof from the ministries of Canning and Goderich. It was unclear how much support there was for Lansdowne and those who took office with him. There were no great parliamentary trials of strength during Canning's ministry which enable us to assess how many Whig MPs supported the government. The position of the renegade Whigs was thus never made completely clear. They were in office but they still received their Whip from Lord Duncannon, not from the Treasury. They were never absorbed into the ministry and were unhappy in their ministerial situations, especially after Canning died. The weak Goderich was a far less effective security for resisting royal influence and for promoting liberal causes than Canning had been. Almost as soon was they had left the party, powerful pressures were put upon them to return to it. A group of aristocratic young Whigs, led by Althorp and including Milton, Tavistock, Ebrington and Lord John Russell, as we saw in the last chapter, was working for the reunification of the party, its greater cohesion, and its establishment in office committed to Parliamentary Reform. Through their efforts the Whigs were reminded of the need not merely for discipline but also for organization. They were thus awakened once again to their traditions of party cohesion and ideological consistency. The experience of office in 1827-8 was a slightly farcical, largely unsuccessful interlude for the party before it reasserted its principles and, most of all, its belief in the reform of Parliament. Those who had taken office found themselves discredited and their influence consequently declined. Before long different counsels would be prevailing within the Whig party.

When Wellington replaced Goderich in January 1828 it appeared that the normal pattern of two-party politics was being restored. The ministry even made some show of continuing the characteristic policies of the early 1820s, economic and fiscal reform while maintaining an unyielding attitude towards the reform of the constitution of the country. But the traditional pattern of two-party politics could not now be completely restored. There was no Liverpool to keep the ministry together and no Canning to maintain its public reputation. While the pressure of events forced the ministry to give way on Repeal and Emancipation, these concessions shattered Wellington's coalition and, in the end, rendered him incapable of governing.

It did not take Wellington long to dispense with the services of the Canningites, now led by Huskisson, even if he then proceeded to implement their policies on Repeal and Emancipation. They wished to admit the principle of Parliamentary reform by exchanging the corrupt boroughs of Penryn and East Retford for the large, unrepresented towns of Manchester and Birmingham. Wellington and the rest of the government endeavoured to negotiate a compromise but the Canningites voted against it in the Commons. Wellington had outraged the Ultras by taking in the Canningites. He had been wearied by constant bickering in the cabinet over foreign and economic policy between the left and the right. Now he took advantage of Huskisson's offer of resignation to rid himself of the troublesome Canningite party.

A Tory administration without the Canningites was now in power.

It was in power but it lacked the strength to command events and to control Parliament. The events of the next few months, indeed, amounted almost to a process of reluctant self-liquidation. On the two symbolic issues of Repeal and Emancipation, the government of Wellington was unable to stem the liberal tide. It is, indeed, doubtful if any government could have done so. Repeal, for example, was championed by a powerful alliance of extra-parliamentary Dissenters with a strong, national organization. The measure was proposed by Russell in the Commons and supported by the bulk of the Whig opposition. They argued the by now traditional Whig case that the Test and Corporation Acts belonged to the conditions of the seventeenth not the nineteenth centuries and that for generations the Protestant Dissenters had shown themselves to be loyal and industrious citizens. The offending statutes were hardly ever enforced and stood as anachronistic and symbolic insults to a large minority of the population. What was the point of keeping the legislation on the statute book? The government bowed to the will of the majority and to the mood of the moment and, reversing its early opposition to the measure, actually allowed Peel to pilot the legislation through the Commons. With an even more emphatic collapse of the will to resist, the bench of bishops in the House of Lords overwhelmingly supported the bill. The ghost of Canning must have smiled to witness these contortions of Wellington's ministry.

Not the least important of the consequences of Repeal was that it brought Catholic Emancipation very much closer. Emancipation Bills had in fact passed the Commons in 1823 and 1828 but had been lost in the Lords. Individuals on the government side, notably Canning, had long embraced it. The opposition had been committed to it for a generation. The real obstacles to Emancipation were to be found at court and in the upper chamber. The Repeal showed that resistance was crumbling there. Events in Ireland now enabled such resistance as remained to be overcome.

The suppression of the Irish rebellion of 1798 had led to the incorporation of Ireland within the United Kingdom. The Act of Union of 1801 wound up the Irish Parliament and gave Ireland 100 MPs at Westminster. It had been Pitt's intention to accompany the Act of Union with an Emancipation Bill which would enable Catholics to sit in Parliament. George III had blocked Emancipation then and he continued to do so for the rest of his political life, as indeed did his successor. Thereafter, while the issue hung fire, the commitment of the Whig opposition to Emancipation was accompanied by the gradual conversion of majority opinion in the House of Commons. At the same time, agitation for Emancipation began to spread in Ireland. Daniel

O'Connell founded the Catholic Association in 1823, an impressive and well organized pressure group. Almost as serious, rioting and tumult began to spread. The general election of 1826 made it clear that while No Popery (i.e. resistance to Catholic claims) remained a powerful cry in English politics, in Ireland the elections demonstrated the power of O'Connell and the priests. Hoping for justice from the Canningites, O'Connell held his fire.

The resignation of the Canningites from Wellington's ministry in May 1828 brought matters to a head. The ministerial appointments caused a bye-election at Clare. Realizing that he had nothing to expect of Wellington, O'Connell determined upon a trial of strength. His own victory against Wellington's sitting member threatened civil war in Ireland. If he, O'Connell, as a Catholic, was not allowed to take his seat then the subsequent disorders might threaten the Union. Certainly, Britain did not have the military power to occupy Ireland. Yet the only alternative to the coercion of the Catholic Association was Emancipation. There was no half-way house. To call a general election would arouse anti-Catholic feeling in England while throwing British rule in Ireland into question. Wellington came to the conclusion that Emancipation must be conceded. In doing so, he was repudiating the *raison d'être* of his own ministry. Nevertheless, throwing the weight of his reputation and the power of the government behind it, he was able to rush an Emancipation Bill through both Houses in March-April 1829.[11]

There can be no question that Emancipation was one of the greatest shocks to the Tory party in its entire history. There was now little left in common between the Canningites, at one extreme, the Ultras, at the other and those who had, in the end, reluctantly embraced Emancipation, Wellington and Peel. With the benefit of hindsight, we can see that the forces opposed to parliamentary reform were beginning to lose their cohesion. Even the monarchy, it now appeared, with the assistance of a well organized extra-parliamentary movement or threat, could be coerced. Whatever their historic reputations, Wellington and Peel were hated and distrusted in their party in the aftermath of Emancipation.

The bitterness was of quite extraordinary proportions. 198 MPs and 116 Peers voted against Emancipation. Although they were a mixed bag, Wellington could no longer rely on the loyalty of a large section of

[11] Since 1793 the Irish Catholics (or at least some of them) had enjoyed the right to vote but not to hold office or to sit in Parliament. The Act of 1829 opened all offices, except those of Viceroy and Chancellor, to Catholics. It is worth adding that the Act switched the franchise from the 40 s. freeholder (as in the English counties) to the £10 House-holder. The intention was clearly to weaken O'Connell's influence over the Irish electorate. The malleability of the electoral system, however, was no doubt noted by many an English reformer.

his party. In mid 1829 over 200 Brunswick Clubs sprang into existence in England and Ireland to defend the existing constitution, or what was left of it. By the end of the year the Ultras were on the way to becoming a party within a party. They comprised a majority of Tory Peers, a large minority of Tory MPs, the Brunswick Clubs and, by 1830, over 300 Orange Lodges on this side of the Irish Sea alone. Furthermore, they enjoyed the support of the party press and, to a considerable extent, of George IV. The Ultras were threatening to convert the all-inclusive Toryism of Liverpool, Peel and Wellington into a narrow, coherent, well organized and popularly supported anti-reform Tory party. It may have been too late to stop Parliamentary Reform by now but a majority of the Ultras were determined that the Tory party would have no part in it. Over 2,000 anti-Emancipation petitions had been raised in 1828–9 from the machinery of Brunswick Clubs, Orange Lodges, Pitt Clubs and election committees which together constituted the jumble of Ultra party machinery. There was no knowing what they might achieve on Parliamentary Reform.

This is not to diminish the importance of those in the Tory party who now actually turned to Parliamentary Reform on the grounds that an electoral system which fairly represented the popular will could never have passed Emancipation. Such men, however, were always in the minority. Less than half of the Ultra Tory County MPs (29 in all) supported Parliamentary Reform. Nevertheless, their mentality is significant. They nostalgically believed that the landed interest was no longer fairly dealt with under nor adequately represented in a Parliament selected by government influence, aristocratic proprietors and radical demagogues. The consequence was that the system must be changed. This diversion of Tory energy at a crucial moment was to be of the greatest psychological and numerical assistance to the Whig government of Grey in 1831.

The Whigs were, of course, the natural beneficiaries of these Tory traumas. Emancipation had not been a party victory but it had owed something to their efforts and to their consistency. Furthermore, it had removed their greatest single defining characteristic. With Repeal and Emancipation out of the way, only their predilection for Parliamentary Reform remained to be tested. In the short term, Repeal and the Emancipation crisis had forced the Whigs once more to work together after their recent divisions. Nevertheless, there remained a wide range of opinions within the party on the subject of co-operation with the government. A small trickle of individuals took office under Wellington but it signified little. The bulk of the Whig party hung together even if it lacked the strength as yet even to attempt to bring down the ministry of Wellington and to replace it with a reform administration. That point had not yet been reached.

The Wellington ministry was able to limp on, supported with noticeably little relish by the Tories and opposed as yet with equally little
vigour by the Whigs. The situation was fraught with uncertainty.
Whigs and radicals urged Wellington on to further reforms. The
ministry, looking to its backbenchers, refused to embarrass itself
further. If Wellington were to survive, he needed a period of calm and
tranquillity in which the passions so lately aroused might be allowed to
subside.

The economic distress of 1830 provoked a scenario of distress and
agitation which made it impossible for the political situation to settle.
Clamours for parliamentary reform were growing and, indeed, other
reforms as well, currency reform and the repeal of the Corn Laws
among them. Reform, in short, was still on the agenda. The example
which the ministry had given over Repeal and Emancipation had been
quickly noticed in the country. The death of George IV on 26 June
1830 unsettled an already disturbed political situation in at least two
further respects. It removed the royal veto on Grey and the Whigs,
thus weakening the security of Wellington's ministry. Furthermore,
because a general election had to be held within six months of a royal
demise it opened up the political and parliamentary establishment to
popular influences.

Such was the nature of the electoral system, of course, that the
election held in August 1830 cannot be regarded as anything like a
completely valid test of public opinion. As usual, only one quarter of
constituencies were contested. As usual, elections were an amalgam of
local issues, local personalities and locally organized pressure upon
electors. As usual, the politics of new members was not at once apparent, many of them waiting, no doubt, for the meeting of Parliament to
clarify the uncertain political scene. Nevertheless, there can be little
doubt that the tide of reform was swelling. Although it is unusually
difficult to estimate gains and losses in 1830[12] there can be no denying
the strength of reformist sentiment in the country. There were some
outstanding victories for the Whigs – Brougham swept Yorkshire like
a forest fire in the biggest sensation of the election – and there can be
no denying the lack of enthusiasm for the government. Of the 17 new
county MPs who entered the House in 1830 15 were to vote against the
government in November. Even more remarkable was the dissatisfaction expressed for the prevailing electoral system in many places.
Attacks on established interests – even where these did not proceed as
far as a contest – elicited considerable distaste for proprietorial
politics. It was, even so, less the strength of radical sentiment which is

[12] For what it is worth, the government lost between 10 and 15 seats, the opposition
gained 25 to 30 seats. This estimate can only be made, however, with the benefit of hindsight and once MPs had demonstrated their loyalties *after* Parliament met.

so remarkable in 1830 than the absence of any serious opposition to it. Although the Whigs did not on the whole suffer from this sentiment in 1830 they can hardly have been unaware of it. Indeed, as the debates on the Reform Act were to illustrate, the Whigs did not interpret reformist opinion in the country as a passing wind blown up by the French Revolution of July 1830, still less as a result of allegedly malicious conspiracies of the radicals. They saw in it a profound shift in the sentiments of the middling orders and one which they believed was likely to be permanent.

Wellington was meanwhile preoccupied with keeping his government in existence. To this end he had attempted to reopen his contacts with the Canningites in 1830. In September, however, Huskisson died and at once the future allegiance of the Canningites was thrown into question. Their spokesmen, both future Prime Ministers, Melbourne and Palmerston, had learned the lesson of the general election. They had been impressed with the seriousness of reforming opinion in the country and were by now prepared to contemplate the reform of parliament, something which Canning would never have accepted. Their refusal to take office without the Whigs threw Wellington back upon the Ultras. But it was too late to bring them back into the fold. They still smarted with resentment at Emancipation. To make matters worse, the government had prosecuted the Ultra-Tory newspaper *The Morning Journal* for its libellous attacks on ministers in the autumn of 1829. Some of them, indeed, led by Sir Richard Vyvyan in the summer of 1829, concocted a scheme for getting rid of Wellington and Peel. There was no possibility that they would support the government.

There is no wonder, then, that Wellington failed to reinforce his administration with Canningites and Ultras. His endeavours to do so, however, his appeals to party unity and his desire to strengthen what he called 'the party of government' are most instructive. At the same time, while there is no mystery surrounding the failure of his attempts to mollify the Ultras and the Canningites, there did exist the basis for unity among the Tories, once the Canningites had gone over to reform. The Tories had, after all, consistently opposed the Reform of Parliament. During the ministry of Liverpool, many Tories had liberalized their opinions on foreign policy, on trade, on finance and on many social questions. But they had never given an inch on Parliamentary Reform and they had never acquiesced in any of even the most moderate of schemes of reform. For this there was a good reason. The Tories controlled three times as many of the patronage boroughs as the Whigs. It was a tragedy for the Tory party that the bitterness of Emancipation made reconciliation on reform impossible. Ironically, it was Wellington's famous statement on 2 November 1830 that the constitution was perfect, required no improvement and possessed the confidence of the people which proved the undoing of his government. In the face of mounting distress and rising political agitation in the country it was an astonishing declaration. The enemies of the ministry – Whig, Radical, Ultra and Canningite – moved in for the kill. Brougham was to move a Parliamentary Reform motion on 16 November 1830. The day before the ministry attempted to oppose a motion for a select committee on Civil List expenditure.[13] It lost by 233 to 204. The next day Wellington's government resigned.

Between Catholic Emancipation and the fall of Wellington's government changes of critical importance had been taking place within the Whig party and which facilitated its acceptance of office in November 1830. Up to the 1830 session, however the Whig leaders had not been conspicuously united nor had they been outspoken in their advocacy of Parliamentary Reform. To some extent, they were suspicious of the reform agitation, looked to Wellington to contain it and were reluctant to attack him in case his very real weaknesses caused George IV to replace him with an Ultra-Tory government. Nevertheless, the sheer pressure of events could not fail to have some impact upon the Whigs. On 23 February 1830 Russell's motion to enfranchise Manchester, Leeds and Birmingham was lost by only 188 to 140. On this occasion, the Whigs enjoyed the support of the Canningites; their political position was perceptibly strengthening and with it their morale and self-confidence.

Their greatest single weakness in recent years had been feeble leadership. For over a decade the party had not had a Leader in the House of Commons. It was in March 1830 that about 40 Whig MPs petitioned Althorp to assume the Leadership and this he agreed to do. Soon over 100 MPs had associated themselves with this development and, shortly afterwards, the whole party. Meanwhile, Lord Grey himself was beginning to take a more active role in politics than for years past.

It would be misleading to accept Grey on the valuation of the Whig historians of the nineteenth century. Far from being the man of destiny awaiting the call of history to carry a Bill to reform Parliament, he had spent the past year awaiting an offer of place and power in Wellington's administration. Place may have been on offer. Power was not. Gradually, Grey began to assert his eminently Whiggish qualities when he reappeared in London in April 1830. The heir of Fox and the life-long campaigner for the reform of Parliament, he managed to combine the appearance of calm statesmanship with an almost

---

[13] Of 60 leading Ultras only 9 voted for the government, 34 Tories voted against the government, five more than the margin of its defeat. There is, of course, some possibility that the ministry could have survived Brougham's motion had it stayed to fight.

distracted concern for the preservation of law, order and property. He attacked Wellington's refusal to contemplate reform and his feebleness in the face of popular agitation. Lord Grey was rapidly reaching the conclusion that Wellington's government was beginning to threaten not merely the prospects of reform but even the peace and security of the country.

Vigour and leadership had thus been restored when the death of George IV on 26 June 1830 ended the proscription from which the Whig party had been suffering for a generation. Even before the King's death, Grey had decided upon an attack on Wellington's ministry. Now he need feel few inhibitions about doing so. Angered by William IV's unthinking continuation of Wellington in office, the disappointed Grey moved his party up to make a formal assault on the ministry. In the event, Wellington was defeated by a combination of groups, not by an exclusively party effort. The Whigs and the Canningites were joined by a small number of radicals, a few Irish MPs under O'Connell's leadership, a small number of Ultras and a few other disaffected Tories. No wonder there was talk among contemporaries that party distinctions were a thing of the past. Of course, they were mistaken. The reform issue was creating a temporary confusion of parties but the Ultras and the Tories were to return to their natural home before 1832. On the Whig side, a more significant realignment of party groupings was taking place but it was less than momentous. The Whig party was about to absorb the Canningites but the Radicals and the Irish were to remain its less than comfortable bed-fellows long after 1832. In November 1830, this broad coalition of groups effected the destruction of Wellington's government.

Most historians have seized on the inclusive structure of Grey's cabinet, noting its aristocratic personnel and the generosity shown to the Canningites. Although the Canningites numbered only about a dozen in each House, they took three Secretaryships of State and the Board of Control. In addition, a few Tories, including the Ultra Duke of Richmond in the cabinet, obtained places. There is something to be said, therefore, for the view that regards Grey's ministry as something less than an exclusively party ministry. Nevertheless, the Whigs took almost all of the other offices.[14] The Canningites were permanently incorporated. And it was not long after reform was achieved that the non-Whig office holders were shed. Grey's ministry was not therefore

<hr>

[14] 'Yet though it was a coalition, Grey's administration was still essentially Whig. The leaders in the Lords and Commons were Whigs, the leading figures of the party took office in it, the bulk of its support came from the old Whig party. The principles on which it was founded, reform, retrenchment and peace were Whig principles; and people at large called it a Whig government.' A. Mitchell, *The Whigs in Opposition*, p. 248.

initially a party ministry. After all, reform had to be carried and the government had to survive. Within two years, however, it had become a party ministry. By then the confusion of parties had given way to a renewal of two-party politics.

Conclusion: The Reform Act of 1832 and the British Party System

The Reform Crisis of 1831–2 heightened party activity while deepening public involvement in the political conflict at Westminster. Tory resistance to reform provoked an enormous reaction of support for the ministry of Grey. The battle for the Reform Act was waged between two well organized armies, fighting for distinct political objectives and contending for the support of the public.

Both parties were bound to be affected by the conflict. The Whigs had to accustom themselves to the unfamiliar experience of ministerial responsibility, the Tories to the cold winds of opposition. After the fall of Wellington the Tories were no longer the party of the Crown and, as events were to prove, no longer the natural party of government. They proceeded, not without enormous hesitation and reluctance, to form themselves into an organized opposition party which resisted both the men and the measures of a government which had been approved by the King. Wellington and Peel, however, disliked forcing the King's hand and were unwilling to displace ministers of the King's (and of the public's) choice. Although there was little prospect of their being able to form a viable government in the conditions of 1831–2, the Tory party's opposition to reform marks the final acceptance of the idea of a 'loyal opposition', the final indispensable condition for a two-party system. Further, the introduction of the First Reform Bill into the House of Commons in March 1831 marks the moment of truth for the Tories. Its surprisingly far-reaching proposals terrified not only the Ultras but Tory opinion in general.[1] Thereafter, all shades of opinion within the party, whatever their past differences, were all ready for reconciliation.

Liberated from the responsibilities of office, the Tory party was able to complete the final stages of its emergence as an autonomous Tory

---

[1] It was fortunate for the Tories that those Ultras who embraced parliamentary reform did so with such tactical ineptness that they destroyed themselves. They accepted reform but opposed Grey's bills. Thus they alienated reforming opinion and offended the Tories. Inevitably, they came to grief at the elections of 1831 and 1832. The Ultra party may thus be said to have come to an end in 1832 although its spirit continued to haunt the Tory party for many a day.

party, as distinct from a party of government. Its organizational structure had hitherto been closely identified with ministerial influence and government offices. It is, moreover, widely assumed that the Tories did not develop autonomous party institutions until after the Reform Act. In fact, such institutions came into existence while the Tories were resisting reform. Within weeks of the fall of Wellington's ministry a committee had sprung up to manage the fortunes of the Tory party in Parliament from a house in Charles Street. The 'Charles Street Gang' sent notices to MPs, dealt with the London and provincial press and began to manage bye-elections. Its expenses were met partly out of a party fund and partly out of Members' subscriptions. During the general election of 1831 the 'gang' found much to do, supplying candidates with constituencies, constituencies with candidates and supplying both with money. Early in 1832 the Carlton Club had replaced Charles Street as the central party headquarters.[2] The Carlton, unlike Brooks, was essentially a Club for party and political purposes. Initially it brought together Tories of all shades opposed to the Reform Bill. Its future role was to be more far-reaching. Nevertheless, the organizational foundations of the post-Reform Tory party were being completed.

Indeed, there was much for it to do. The Reform Act weakened the electoral strength of the Tory party, although it was able to retain its traditional domination of the counties. Paradoxically, the Tories, if anything, *strengthened* their hold on the House of Lords after 1832. The Reform Crisis drove the bench of bishops solidly into their arms. This coincided with the virtual disappearance of the Party of the Crown in the House of Lords. In the 1830s almost all Peers were receiving a Whip from one party or the other. This movement of the peers once and for all into the parties did much to preserve and to prolong the political influence of their order. Independent Peers were after 1832 almost as rare as Independent MPs.

The ministry of Lord Grey, as we have seen, was not a pure party ministry although it was dominated by the Whigs. During the next few years, as politicians adjusted themselves to the new and sometimes confusing conditions created by the Reform Act, old and new party institutions served to define the party's membership and to strengthen its public support. It is most significant that the Whigs did not rely solely upon the customary attractions of ministerial influence for their following and their coherence. In office, they were prepared to be firm with the monarch. The decision to dissolve Parliament in 1831 and the threat to create peers were both forced upon an unwilling William IV. The recognition that office could be sustained by party rather than by

[2] The Carlton Club is usually taken to be the organizational focus of the Tory party between the Reform Act and the 1870s.

royal favour may be seen in its establishment of the Whig answer to the Carlton Club, the Reform Club, opened in 1836. The timing is significant. Their great victories at the elections of 1831 and 1832 appeared to render superfluous any further organizational initiatives on the part of the Whigs. Tory successes at the election of 1835 made them think again. The Reform, however, did little more than place upon a more systematic and prestigious basis those functions which had been undertaken by earlier, less formal types of party organization. The type, although not the extent, of party activity undertaken by the Reform marks little advance upon the work of William Adam in the 1780s. Nevertheless, the scope and ambition, and to some extent the bureaucratic efficiency of the undertaking, deserve recognition.

It was, indeed, an important consequence of the Reform Act to extend established patterns of party activity to new quarters. The newly enfranchised towns and the somewhat artificially divided county constituencies developed the apparatus of party with an ease and rapidity which was sometimes astonishing. There were, of course, exceptions. Informal methods of political control were sufficient to manage many county seats in England and Wales and a few of the smaller boroughs as well, to delay the appearance of local party institutions and to defer the intervention of central party institutions for another generation.[3]

One of the most dramatic consequences of the Reform Act upon party development in Britain was the opening up of politics in Scotland. Most Scottish counties and boroughs had been so oligarchic and so closely controlled from London that Scottish MPs before 1832 constituted a silent battalion of government supporters. Nowhere was the Reform Bill more enthusiastically greeted than in the northern kingdom. In spite of powerful currents of intellectual Whiggism centred on Edinburgh, party had made little impact either upon the Scottish electorate or upon Scottish MPs before 1832. (With a pre-1832 electorate of 5,000 for a total of 30 counties and 66 burghs it is hardly surprising.)[4] Although the new counties remained liable to the influence of patrons (their average electorate was little over 1,000 – sharply less than their English counterparts) many grateful Scottish seats swung to the Scottish Whig party in the 1830s, which was

[3] Ireland remained to a large extent outside the framework of party evolution in the rest of the United Kingdom. There had been signs of an Irish version of Foxite Whiggism in the 1780s and 1790s but Whiggism had been overtaken by Catholicism and by Nationalism. Catholics had been allowed to vote since 1793 and inevitably, election issues, especially in the Irish counties, were heavily imbued with religious considerations. Once Emancipation allowed Catholics to become MPs, however, the nationalist and to some extent economic issues of Ireland finally overshadowed the traditional battle between Whigs and Tories at Westminster.

[4] After 1832 the Scottish electorate numbered 65,000.

efficiently managed from Edinburgh. The new burghs averaged 1,300 electors, a fairly respectable size, and were sufficiently considerable to absorb and reflect liberal opinions. Although the new franchises were open to abuse and amenable to influence, such games could now be played by Whigs as well as Tories. Interestingly, the most faithful government supporters before 1832 had been from Scotland and, until Emancipation, from Ireland. After 1832 the Toryism of the English and Welsh counties and small boroughs was to be offset by the liberalism of Scotland and, on certain issues, that of Ireland.

The extension of the franchise in 1832 unmistakably created a new environment in which the parties had to work. Consequently, their functions underwent changes of no little significance. After 1832 it became generally – and permanently – assumed that both government and opposition must rest upon a party basis. Cabinet government gives way to government based on party, to which is opposed an opposition based on party. Furthermore, political life was now dominated by powerful party organizations with vital electoral purposes, viz. to win a majority of seats and to obtain or to retain control of the government. In other words, the need to implement the Reform Act created a set of possibilities for both parties to which their response was a competitive appeal to the constituencies.

Both great parties were forced by necessity, therefore, to attract the support of new elements in the political scene while retaining or recapturing that of established interests. They were forced to mount an effective appeal to vast sections of the nation. Significantly, the old names, Whig and Tory, while they lingered on to describe political types and temperaments, were no longer used to define party alignments. The words 'Liberal' and 'Conservative', popularized in the struggle for reform in 1831–2, were now coming into common usage to describe the government and the opposition parties of the mid 1830s. The change is significant. It represents the old Whig party's commitment to the idea of liberal progress. At the same time, it represents the old Tory party's recognition of the need for ordered change and progress while conserving the essential heritage of the British constitution and British institutions. After Catholic Emancipation and after the Reform Act, no serious alternative was available to the Tories.

We should be cautious, however, of hailing a new start to party politics in the 1830s. Most historians have detected significant continuities before and after Reform. The historian of party is positively embarrassed with them. Even the great political upheavals of 1827–32 had failed to shatter the old groupings. The Canningites changed their allegiance, it is true, and the loyalties of others were severely tested and even seriously disturbed but when the dust had settled the old parties were seen to have survived remarkably well. Furthermore, the new political energies unleashed by the Reform Act, especially in the new constituencies and in Scotland, were contained remarkably effectively within the existing two-party framework. Although the arrival of new issues after 1832 needs to be carefully noted, the continuing force of the old issues – of religion, of free trade and, indeed, of reform – hardly needs to be emphasized. Some historians have argued that party alignments came to dominate the House of Commons after 1834–5. If by this they mean that the party allegiances of the 250 + new MPs elected in 1832 needed several years to emerge then they are, of course, perfectly correct. But party alignments as such had dominated Parliament since the end of the Napoleonic Wars.[5] Similarly, it is not easy to see that a more stable party system emerged after 1832. The Repeal of the Corn Laws disrupted the stability and cohesion of parties in 1846. Nor were the post-1832 parties significantly more cohesive than their predecessors. The divisions in the Whig party between 1832 and 1841 are sufficient to dispose of this idea. Those in the Tory party after 1846, and possibly even earlier, are even more instructive.

Likewise, the inspiration for the impressive burst of extra-parliamentary party activity which is normally assumed to have followed the Reform Act in fact antedates it. The great radical ground-swell of 1830–2 spawned associations and organizations in places which had never known them before. Local organizations sprang up where they did not exist and were revivified where they did. Of course, the Registration clauses of the Reform Bill ensured that permanent local party associations needed to be established but these often existed already, sometimes in more than embryonic form. Furthermore, the significance of the experiments in central direction of party affairs, in the shape of the Carlton and Reform Clubs, should not be overestimated. These central party institutions effected little or no fundamental shift of power from the constituencies to a London-based party machine. They systematized the sometimes uncoordinated activities of earlier, somewhat informal, bodies but they do not mark any qualitative change in the nature of party politics. In some places, the new clubs did not survive for very long, especially once the new electoral circumstances which obtained after 1832 were seen to benefit one party overwhelmingly. In others, of course, where the power of patrons continued to be considerable, especially in the counties, party was much inferior to social and economic considerations in its political influence.

Central clubs and party managers still had very limited functions and very limited powers. Their function was to provide some elements of common purpose and direction for local parties. They could not dictate to these local groups so long as they operated on a financial shoestring and so long as the power to return a member depended upon local rather than upon national considerations. They could help them to find candidates and could provide information and propaganda but could only offer small amounts of money.[6] In any case, their activities touched only a minority of constituencies. In the majority, money was locally raised and locally expended. In the Liberal party, indeed, one half of MPs did not belong to the Reform Club. These national clubs could bestow the badge of orthodoxy upon local aspirants but they lacked the coercive abilities to impose their will upon them. Whatever their precise long-term significance, the central party institutions of the 1830s do not represent a new departure in the evolution of the two-party system; rather they represent the accommodation of that system to the particular circumstances of politics after the First Reform Act.

Although it cannot be denied that party remained for the Victorians – as to some extent it does today – a faintly discreditable phenomenon, the custom of thinking about politics instinctively in two-party terms had become securely established by 1832. (The fact that the confusion of parties between 1827 and 1832 was so much remarked upon by contemporaries tells its own story.) By this time, politicians and political writers had come to fashion the past in accordance with party ideologies, to develop in short, rival interpretations of British history since the seventeenth century in terms of the party labels and party principles of the present. Already, the idea that through the agency of party electors were being presented with a choice of government, and with it a choice of party programmes, had made its appearance. The essential ingredients of the British two-party system had, indeed, not only appeared but had been largely accepted both by politicians and by public opinion by 1832.

[6] More research needs to be done on the financing of party organizations. It is doubtful, however, if either party ever had more than £50,000 with which to fight a general election. After the payment of incidental expenses, subsidies to the press and writers of pamphlets, there can have been little more than a few hundred pounds for each constituency.

Select Bibliography.

General Works

Recent text-books have been considerably more sophisticated than their predecessors in their analysis of party politics. John B. Owen, *The Eighteenth Century, 1714-1815* (Nelson, 1974) [chapters 5 and 12] provides the political and constitutional background. The more conventional surveys of events in two further works are of a high quality. A. Briggs, *The Age of Improvement* (Longmans, 1959) has worn extremely well. It has not been superseded even by the excellence of Professor N. Gash's *Aristocracy and People, 1815-1865*. (Edward Arnold, 1979) The earlier volume in this series, Professor I.R. Christie, *Wars and Revolutions, 1760-1815*, had not appeared when this volume went to press.

The Revival of the Whig Party

A considerable literature has accumulated in the last few decades on the Whig party. At one time, it was fashionable to deny the importance of party combination in late eighteenth-century politics. See, for example, L.B. Namier, *Crossroads of Power* (1962); J. Brooke, *The Chatham Administration, 1766-68* (Macmillan, 1956, chapters 6-7). More recently, greater attention has been paid to the Rockingham Whigs in particular. See Frank O'Gorman, *The Rise of Party in England, 1760-82*, (Allen and Unwin, 1975). John Brewer has interestingly investigated their public statements and their ideological significance in *Party Ideology and Popular Politics at the Accession of* George III, (CUP, 1977) while John Derry has provided an elegant and convenient summary of current views of the Rockinghams and their age in *English Politics and the American Revolution* (Dent, 1976). The philosophy of Burke is briefly discussed in Frank O'Gorman, *Edmund Burke: His Political Philosophy*, (Allen and Unwin, 1973).

The constitutional crisis of 1782-84 is wittily and concisely dealt with in J. Cannon, *The Fox-North Coalition: Crisis of the Constitution, 1782-84* (CUP, 1969) The development of the Whig party thereafter is treated in Frank O'Gorman, *The Whig Party and the French Revolution* (Macmillan, 1967); L.G. Mitchell, *Charles James Fox and the Disintegration of the Whig Party, 1782–94* (OUP, 1971); John W. Derry, *The Regency Crisis and the Whigs, 1788–89* (CUP, 1963); Donald E. Ginter, *Whig Organisation in the General Election of 1790* (University of California Press, 1967). Most of the above works attach rather too much significance to their own area of study. Derry, for example, in my view exaggerates the role of the Regency Crisis in Whig realignment; Ginter overestimates the importance of Adam's party institutions; Mitchell treats Fox as possessed of more political cunning and tactical skill than I can recognize.

After 1794 useful literature on the Whigs is much harder to find. Much of the best work is in unpublished dissertations. The general reader may find the relevant sections of A.S. Foord, *His Majesty's Opposition, 1714–1832* (OUP, 1964) a useful introduction. Clive Emsley, *British Society and the French Wars, 1793–1815* (Macmillan, 1979) has achieved a miracle of compression but he does not have much to say about the Foxites. A. Harvey, *British Society in the Early nineteenth Century*, despite its title and despite its tendency to pontificate, has little save narrative detail about the Whig party in the early years of the new century. It is, therefore, lack of opposition, as well as its own merits, which enables Michael Roberts's pre-war study of *The Whig Party, 1807–12* (Macmillan, 1937) to be recommended. Richard Willis is one of the few historians to have come to grips with the Foxites. His study of 'Fox, Grenville and the Recovery of the Opposition' (*Journal of British Studies*, XI, 1972) is eminently promising.

The Rehabilitation of Toryism.

Here is a subject in need of a historian. Some of the constituent elements in the new Toryism have been dealt with by historians but no synthesis of the larger subject has yet been attempted. The beginning of Tory sentiment out of doors is touched upon in Paul Langford's essay 'Old Whigs, Old Tories and the American Revolution' (in *The British Atlantic Empire before the American Revolution*, eds. P. Marshall and G. Williams (Frank Cass, 1980). Of course, some of the relevant themes are touched upon in works cited above, especially that by Emsley. The work of the Reeves societies may be glimpsed in E.C. Black, *The Association* (Harvard U.P., 1963) and, more controversially, in Donald E. Ginter, 'The Loyalist Association Movement of 1792–93 and British Public Opinion' (*Historical Journal*, IX, 1966). Albert Goodwin's *The Friends of Liberty: the English Democratic Movement in the Age of the French Revolution* (Hutchinson, 1979) deals with loyalist opinion but also with the 'Tory' policies of the government. Emsley also has much to say about this.

The literature on the early political manifestations of the new Toryism is sketchy, to say the least. Much of what there is remains unpublished. The account in A.S. Foord is probably the best that there is. That in Harvey is somewhat less useful. Inevitably, one has recourse to older works and the periodical literature. The old account in Keith Feiling, *The Second Tory Party* (OUP, 1938) may yield something to the discerning investigator. So may *The Age of Grey and Peel* by H.W.C. Davis (OUP, 1924). However, we need more detailed studies like those of Lipscomb and McQuiston (P.C. Lipscomb, 'George Canning and the Trinidad Question', *Historical Journal*, XII, 1969; J. McQuiston, 'Rose and Canning in Opposition, 1806–07', *ibid*. XIV 1971).

The Party System of the Early Nineteenth Century

This may be initially examined in the relevant parts of the neglected and much underestimated work by Alan Beattie, *English Party Politics* (Weidenfeld & Nicholson, 1970). The student may then proceed to Derek Beales masterly essay 'The Independent Member', an essay whose implications go far beyond what is suggested in its title ('Parliamentary Parties and the Independent Member', in R. Robson (ed) *Ideas and Institutions of Victorian Britain* (Bells, 1967). The same author's *The Political Parties of Nineteenth Century Britain* (Historical Association, London, 1971) puts the subject in its proper perspective. There is interesting material in that sometimes neglected goldmine for this period, *English Historical Documents, 1783–1832* ed. by A. Aspinall and E.A. Smith (Eyre & Spottiswoode, 1959). D. Large's article 'The Decline of the Party of the Crown and the Rise of Parties in the House of Lords, 1783–1837' (*English Historical Review*, LXXVIII, 1963) covers a neglected subject but not entirely satisfactorily. Some criticisms may be found in M. McCahill, *Order and Equipoise: (TRHS,* 1978). There is little satisfactory work on the subject of party organization in this period. The standard work is by A. Aspinall (Party Organization in the Early nineteenth Century, *English Historical Review*, XLI 1926) but its age requires it to be updated.

There is a paucity of material on party in the constituencies. In addition to local histories, however, the student may turn to J. Phillips, 'Popular Politics in Unreformed England', *Journal of Modern History,* LII (1980) and the same author's 'The Structure of Electoral Politics in Unreformed England', *Journal of British Studies*, XIX (1980). My own study, *The Unreformed Electorate* will appear in 1983.

The Party Conflict of the Early Nineteenth Century

The standard work on the Whig party in this period is A. Mitchell, *The Whigs in Opposition, 1815–30* (OUP, 1967). A. Aspinall, *Lord Brougham and the Whig Party* (Manchester UP, 1927) is a cautious account of its incautious subject.

This is one of the few periods in which the Tories have attracted greater attention than the Whigs. Professor Gash's treatment of Liverpool's ministry in his text-book (See above) is masterly. Together with the following modern works, it can now be safely concluded that W.R. Brock's *Lord Liverpool and Liberal Toryism* (Frank Cass, 1941) has at last been superseded. J.E. Cookson, *Lord Liverpool's Administration, 1815–22*, (Scottish Academic Press, 1975); Boyd Hilton, *Cash, Corn, Commerce: The Economic Policies of the Tory Governments, 1815–30* (Oxford, 1977); Barry Gordon, *Political Economy in Parliament, 1819–23*, (MacMillan, 1976); and his *Economic Doctrine and Tory Liberalism, 1824–30* (Macmillan, 1979); R. Stewart, *The Foundations of the Conservative Party (1832–67)*, in spite of its terminal dates, has a most useful section on the period before 1832.

The modern treatments of the reform question and the fall of the *ancien régime* are not entirely satisfactory. The relevant chapters of J.A.C. Cannon, *Parliamentary Reform, 1660–1832* (CUP, 1972) are a more balanced and comprehensive treatment than that to be found in the disappointing work by Michael Brock, *The Great Reform Act* (Hutchinson, 1973). There is further interesting discussion of this, and related issues, in Professor Cannon's contribution, 'New Lamps for Old: The End of Hanoverian England' in *The Whig Ascendancy: Colloquies on Hanoverian England*, ed. J. Cannon (Edward Arnold, 1981). The religious issues may be followed in G.I.T. Machin, *The Catholic Question in British Politics* (Clarendon Press, 1964); J. Bossy, *The English Catholic Community, 1570–1850*) (Darton, Longman & Todd, 1975); A.D. Gilbert, *Religion and Society in* Industrial England (Longman) and U. Henriques, *Religious* Toleration in England, 1787–1833 (Routledge & Kegan Paul, 1961).

Conclusion

The interpretation offered in this book conflicts with the accepted or orthodox view that a two-party system was created by the 1832 Reform Act. See, however, N. Gash, *Politics in the Age of Peel*, (Longman, 1953); *Reaction and Reconstruction in English Politics, 1832–52* (Clarendon Press, 1965); G. Kitson-Clark, *The Making of Victorian England* (Methuen, 1962); and his *An Expanding Society, Britain, 1830–1900* (CUP, 1967).

Index